PRAISE

EXPLORING THE MIRACULOUS,
BY MICHAEL O'NEILL

Few if any who are writing about religion today do so with the feeling that Michael O'Neill brings to this vastest of topics. His work is grounded in fact but never disregards the spiritual, as is entirely appropriate. Reading O'Neill, one comes to understand belief and faith in the modern world. His writing informs and inspires; it is smart and steeped in understanding.

— Robert Sullivan, managing editor of LIFE books
and author of *Two Saints, Mary: Blessed Art Thou
Among Women* and *Pope Francis in America.*

Eighty percent of Americans report they believe in miracles. For those who do, and for those who are curious, Michael O'Neill's *Exploring the Miraculous* is a "godsend"! As a Stanford-trained engineer, O'Neill delivers fascinating, scientific, data-driven material to explain the supernatural. His website miraclehunter.com is an invaluable resource for anyone wondering how to put miracles in context, and now *Exploring the Miraculous* goes even deeper to explain the inexplicable.

— Maureen Orth, author of "The Most Powerful Woman
in the World," *National Geographic* cover story
about the Virgin Mary (December 2015)

With the heart of a believer and the mind of a skeptic, O'Neill's *Exploring the Miraculous* is a smart, comprehensive look at the fascinating world of miracles.

— Rev. Francis J. Hoffman (Fr. Rocky),
Executive Director of Relevant Radio

Should we explore the miraculous? Yes! We all need miracles, and we need the insight of the Catholic Church if we are to wholeheartedly embrace authentic miracles. In his wonderful book *Exploring the Miraculous*, Michael O'Neill opens up for us that safe path of Church-inspired direction!

— Fr. Peter R. Stryker, C.P.M., Rector, Shrine of Our Lady of Good Help (the first and only Church-approved Marian apparition site in the United States)

Perhaps it's time to give miracles another look. This is precisely the outstanding opportunity provided by Michael O'Neill in this treasure chest of the legitimately supernatural. In this extraordinarily well-documented study, the author provides optimum historical, theological, medical, and scientific evidence wherever possible in defense and articulation of some of Christian history's best occasions of God's benevolent interference.

— Dr. Mark Miravalle, Professor of Theology and Mariology, Franciscan University of Steubenville

EXPLORING THE
MIRACULOUS

EXPLORING THE
MIRACULOUS

Michael O'Neill

Our Sunday Visitor Publishing Division
Our Sunday Visitor, Inc.
Huntington, Indiana 46750

Nihil Obstat:
Msgr. Michael Heintz, Ph.D.
Censor Librorum

Imprimatur:
✠ Kevin C. Rhoades
Bishop of Fort Wayne-South Bend
October 28, 2015

Our Sunday Visitor Publishing Division, Our Sunday Visitor, Inc., 200 Noll Plaza, Huntington, IN 46750; 1-800-348-2440

ISBN: 978-1-61278-779-4 (Inventory No. T1585)
eISBN: 978-1-61278-958-3
LCCN: 2015943727

Cover design: Amanda Falk
Interior design: Dianne Nelson

Cover images: Rays, Shutterstock; *St. Francis Receiving the Stigmata,* c. 1580 (marble), Pilon, Germain (1535–1590) / Cathedrale Sainte-Croix-Saint-Jean des Armeniens, Paris / © Clement Guillaume / Bridgeman Images.

PRINTED IN THE UNITED STATES OF AMERICA

CONTENTS

FOREWORD

The most definitive theological treatise ever composed on the nature of miracles, mysticism, and revelations was written in the eighteenth century by Cardinal Lambertini, at that time prefect for the Sacred Congregation for Rites and later to become Pope Benedict XIV. The introduction to a partial English translation done by nineteenth-century English Oratorians provides an excellent framework by which to examine and to appreciate the contents of this book:

> The Church began with miracles and divine gifts, and, being one, she continues the same. As the ancient dispensation began with Moses, and was inaugurated with miracles, so it continues from age to age, to the pond of Probatica (cf. Jn 5:2). The dispensation of the gospel is more glorious than that of the law (2 Cor 3:9) and is fulfilled in measure beyond the capacity of its predecessor.... If the miracles of the law ceased not at the death of Moses, and if the record of them is not confined to the Pentateuch, but is continued through the history of kings and prophets, much more are we to expect a similar result in the history of Holy Church. The Acts of the Apostles do but carry on the miraculous record of the Four Gospels; and is there any reason that we should suppose that marvelous gifts, graces, and miracles ceased with the apostolic age? This would be the reasoning of the Sadducees, who confined themselves to the five books of Moses, and disowned the prophets. They had closed their hearts against

the perpetual evidence of their temple, and refused to believe in the interference of God, and His dealings with that economy under which they were living.[1]

Thank God that he does choose to "interfere" with our world. Considering that our entire deposit of Christian revelation has been accompanied by miracles and signs — the Lord's reminder that he is with us and is truly behind this Christian movement of grace — why would we reach a point in the twenty-first century when we have, as a human family, decided that we no longer need such supernatural gifts and, moreover, throw our present skepticism back into history in order to deny all past supernatural interventions?

Since true miracles are intended by God to buttress Christian faith, and since our present age suffers from an extreme privation of faith in the forms of both ubiquitous secular humanism and increasing atheism, perhaps it's time to give miracles another look.

This is precisely the outstanding opportunity provided by Michael O'Neill in this treasure chest of the legitimately supernatural. In this extraordinarily well-documented study, the author provides optimal historical, theological, medical, and scientific evidence wherever possible in defense and articulation of some of Christian history's best occasions of God's benevolent interference.

Certainly, the extreme and the fanatical can be present dangers whenever one claims some event to be of a heavenly cause. Yet to reject miracles outright is not only to throw out the baby with the bath water but, still more troubling, to imply that babies don't exist at all. And if babies don't exist, then what of parents? Yes, a categorical denial of the miraculous can lead to the conclusion of a godless universe.

If you were God and witnessed the present state of human affairs on a global scale, wouldn't you try to help?

Michael O'Neill's study of the supernatural contained in this outstanding text is, in its own right, a type of miracle. No, as the author would be quick, perhaps even frantic, to admit, he is not God and this book is not the result of a direct supernatural intervention. At the same time, this wonderful work points to heaven, calls us to look upward, and stresses the vertical axis of human existence between God and man as a refreshing remedy to the dominant horizontal axis, which has contemporary humanity almost exclusively turned in on itself.

May the purpose of true miracles be achieved in the heart of every reader: greater faith in Jesus, greater love for the Church, greater gratitude for the infinite interferences of God.

Dr. Mark Miravalle
Professor of Theology and Mariology
Franciscan University of Steubenville
May 13, 2015, Memorial of Our Lady of Fátima

PREFACE

One of my favorite miracle stories came from a woman at a summer barbecue I attended. Upon hearing about my work, she pulled me aside and said, "I have an amazing story about my son!" She went on to tell me that she had brought her young son to Mass, and at the Consecration he had raised his eyes to the ceiling and excitedly whispered, "Look, it's the saints! Mom, I can see the saints!" The mother went home and excitedly called all her Catholic-mom friends to brag that her young son was a mystic in the making. During Mass the next Sunday, the woman could hardly concentrate on the liturgy as she kept a watchful eye on her child, in case he should see visions again. He sat quietly during the Mass until the Consecration, when he once again raised his arms and pointed upward excitedly. "Mom, the saints are on the ceiling!" The woman raised her eyes and looked hard, and, sure enough, she saw what the boy saw. Painted on the ceiling was a fleur-de-lis — which happens to be the logo of the NFL's New Orleans Saints. Apparently the woman's young mystic had been watching plenty of football with his father in addition to attending Mass with his mother.

Just what is a miracle anyway? Traditionally the term has meant a mysterious and prodigious fact, an event of divine intervention that cannot be explained scientifically. To the modern educated person, there may be little room for miracles. Such a person might argue that just because something cannot be explained with current knowledge, experience, or scientific investigation, it doesn't mean that there couldn't be an explanation … someday. We don't know what we don't know. Even St. Augustine said in his *City of God* (*De Civitate Dei contra Paganos*), "Miracles are not contrary to nature, but only contrary to what we know about nature." And certainly, some would assert, a lack of answers is hardly proof positive for divine intervention.

The most famous foundation for rejecting the possibility of miracles such as apparitions is the thought of prominent atheist David Hume, who circularly argued that miracles are impossible because miracles cannot happen.[2] As Antony Flew commented while he was still an atheist, "If we were in a position to suppose [there is a God], then no doubt the case for the occurrence of these particular miracles, as well as for that of the supreme miracle of the Resurrection, would be open and shut."[3]

Many people who profess faith in God will contend that the big miracles (or at least the stories of them) happened only in ancient days but that smaller ones — the conversion of a hardened soul or the spontaneous healing of a disease — still may happen. But some of the more magnificent miracle stories (still purported to be happening today around the world) are looked at with suspicion at best. People of faith might find miracles frustratingly mysterious and question whether God is capricious: "Why are miracles given to some people and not to others?"

The strange terms *stigmata, inedia,* and *locutions* — found almost exclusively in the Catholic lexicon —might raise a few eyebrows or inspire an occasional rolling of the eye. Certainly apparitions, like miracles in general, are typically frowned on by scientists, academics, and secular humanists who, according to Fr. Dwight Longenecker, author of *Quest for the Creed*, likely find physical miracles "distasteful" and embarrassing because such miracles are "mad, subversive and unpredictable." And as for visions, especially the alleged appearances of the Blessed Virgin Mary when she comes to the world with messages of peace and love and an occasional apocalyptic warning, atheists and agnostics might want to toss them into the same loony bin as UFOs and Bigfoot. Some Protestants have gone as far as to allege that these apparitions are some form of "Mariolatry" or, worse, devil worship. Some see interest in miracles as an overly pious fanaticism crossing the line of good taste into a twilight zone of religious delusion.

The fact is, miracles are important to each and every one of us. Even skeptics and atheists need to have an explanation for the unexplainable. We all pray (or hope) for miracles of one sort or another. Perhaps we beg God for an impossible comeback in a football game or beseech St. Anthony to help us find that lost wallet or wedding ring. We hope for a dream job or an out-of-our-league spouse, and our last and only resort seems to be some sort of divine intervention. When our loved ones are seriously ill, we approach God in great faith with our desperate plea that their lives might be spared. Sometimes the little coincidences of daily life seem to be miraculous reassurances that we are always under the care, protection, and watchful eye of a loving Father.

Our own miracle stories, big and small, are all woven into the vast tapestry of a faith tradition that embraces supernatural events and celebrates them in ways that we might not even realize. Catholics who wear the Miraculous Medal or the scapular in any of its various colors indirectly recall the time-honored apparitions of the Virgin Mary in which these sacramentals find their origins. When we pray the Rosary, we hark back to the legend that St. Dominic received this devotion in a vision, and if we pray between the decades the Fátima prayer,[4] we remember that those words were given to the child visionaries by Our Lady of the Rosary at Fátima in 1917.

I have had an interest in miracles from a young age. I can remember in 1988 excitedly waiting for my seventh-grade religion teacher to give my class updates on the scientific investigation of the Shroud of Turin and being devastated by the results of the carbon-14 dating that placed the famous relic in the thirteenth century. I have worn a Miraculous Medal and a brown scapular for many years and have visited various apparition sites, shrines, and holy places, beginning with the Holy Land. I have attended beatifications and canonizations of saints, ceremonies witnessing to their heroically virtuous lives, attested to by great miracles. As a miracle researcher, I have interviewed stigmatics and seers, held rosaries that have turned gold, viewed rose petals with holy images emblazoned on them, and examined blessed dirt that reportedly has the power to cure great ills. Although I have never been graced with seeing a vision with my own eyes, I have sat in the presence of others as they claimed to see the Virgin Mary. I have talked with obstinate skeptics and with recipients of inexplicable cures and other miracles. Daily I receive e-mails and hear the personal stories of those who claim to have experienced miracles and others who desperately seek them. The accounts range from the truly unbelievable — the raising of a loved one from the dead — to the absurd — the finding of the face of Christ on the doggie door of a house.

I have been grateful for the opportunity to share the great stories of our Faith with audiences big and small — from women's Rosary groups and gatherings of confraternities to enormous conference rooms packed with Marian devotees. I like to joke that miracle hunting does not pay well monetarily but that it pays big in personal connections and stories. At the end of speaking engagements, I am often approached by people with beautiful stories of the miraculous healing of their loved ones or with photos on their phone of fantastic images of light that they believe is a true miracle from heaven.

Many people approach me with two types of questions: "Whom do I talk to so that I can get my miracle investigated?" or "What will happen with Medjugorje [or with another modern supernatural phenomenon]?" Based on the variety in audience makeup alone, from a living room of simple, faithful devotees piously clutching their rosary beads to a country-club dining hall full of Catholic millionaires dressed to the nines, it seems that miracles resonate with all people of faith. Let's face it — we all need a miracle at one point or another.

There are times at a social gathering when the conversation inevitably turns to the weather or to what everyone does for a living, and with the latter topic, I tend to get wide-eyed stares of shock, curiosity, or bewilderment when I reveal that I am a miracle researcher. Almost universally, however, from the skeptic who asks, "So, have you seen one yet?" to the believer who says, "Do I have a miracle story for you!" almost everyone seems to be fascinated by miracles.

Everyone loves a great miracle story, and the idea that miracles are still happening in the world can be cause for excitement. When I worked in Boston, my secretary once brought me some photos she had snapped of the hospital in Medford. The street was overflowing with people so that traffic had to be stopped. She got out of her car to find out what was going on and saw a mysterious image of Our Lady of Guadalupe forming in a window. (The window was later removed by the hospital to ease the traffic jam, and the pattern was later determined to be the result of condensation.)

The sharing of great stories aside, people commonly ask me how I came to become a miracle researcher. The inspiration for it, like many good inspirations in life, came from my mother when I was a little boy. She told me the story of how her mother had fallen away from the Catholic Faith — even became anti-Catholic — when my mother was young. My mother prayed fervently for the intercession of Our Lady of Guadalupe to help my grandmother. As many people commonly do when they pray desperately, she offered a bargain in exchange. My grandmother, miraculously or not, soon reverted to the Faith and became a model of devotion for her children and later for her grandchildren. Making good on her end of the deal, my mother became a schoolteacher when she grew up and taught her students and her own children the beautiful story of the apparitions of Our Lady of Guadalupe each year on her feast day, December 12. The story became a favorite of mine and brought me to consider the Guadalupe story to be the second greatest story ever told. Ever since then, apparitions were of keen interest to me and later materialized in my studies.

When I attended Stanford University, I took a break from my engineering major and science classes and enrolled in an archaeology class. Our final assignment was to identify a famous artifact and write on its significance. Much to the curiosity of my secular professor, I chose to explore the miraculous tilma of Our Lady of Guadalupe. In the process of my research and many hours in the library, I uncovered the rich history of miracles in the Catholic Faith. I had heard of the visions at Guadalupe, Lourdes, and Fátima but had no idea of the number of incredible reports of visions in the tradition of our Faith: more than 2,500 apparitions have been claimed by people of all walks of life from every corner of the globe. After I finished this college paper, I promised myself to return to this study someday, as I found it absolutely fascinating that so many people were making these claims and that the Church actually would risk its credibility to declare any of them worthy of belief.

At the end of my senior year of college, I received from Condoleezza Rice, the vice provost of the school at the time, a piece of advice that I will never forget: *Become an expert in something.* I took it to heart and sought to identify something I was passionate about, something I could learn as much about as possible, and most importantly, something that would bring me closer to God.

As a result, I put my energies into investigating the miracles of the Church.

After more hours of study and research than I can ever recount or care to admit, I combined my scientific curiosity, my engineering-minded love of data, and my professional skills in graphic design and sought to produce the world's top online resource on Marian apparitions: MiracleHunter.com. Now, more than fifteen years later, I am blessed that my research has opened many doors for me, and I consider the inspiration of my mother that led me to my Mother in heaven to be the beginning of it all.

CHAPTER 1

Are Miracles Really
All That Important?

The Church has been enriched by the fruits of miracles from its very beginning. It was the miracles of Christ that invited people to follow him, and it was history's greatest miracle — his resurrection — that changed the world forever. The apostles were emboldened by his mandate to work miracles and the prodigy of Pentecost that sent them on their way into the world. St. Paul's life-altering vision put him on the path to become Christianity's greatest evangelist, and the Roman emperor Constantine was first inspired to legalize Christianity in the year 312 after witnessing a vision in the sky of the IHS Christogram.[5] Miracles big and small surround us, including the greatest one that happens every hour of every day in every country of the world: the Eucharist, bread and wine transformed into Christ's body and blood, which has remained at the center of the Catholic Faith since its institution. The Catholic Church has always affirmed the importance of miracles and revelation and teaches that Christ's works demonstrate that "the kingdom has already arrived on earth."[6]

In many places in Scripture we are able to reflect on the role of the supernatural in our lives of faith. St. Paul, in writing to the Thessalonians, reminds the faithful to be open to miracles: "Do not quench the Spirit, do not despise prophesying, but test everything; hold fast what is good" (1 Thess 5:19–21). Christ worked many miracles of healing, but he did not seem to encourage the search for miracles: "An evil and adulterous generation seeks for a sign, but no sign shall be given to it except the sign of Jonah" (Mt 16:4). In the parable of Lazarus and the rich man, Christ announces that no messenger from the next world will be sent to the brothers of the rich man to encourage them to repent. "If they do not hear Moses and the prophets, neither will they be convinced if some one should rise from the dead" (Lk 16:31). Finally, Christ's words to Thomas are as relevant today as they were when the apostle touched Christ's wounded side: "You have believed because you have seen me. Blessed are those who have not seen and yet believe" (Jn 20:29).

The Catholic Church acknowledges that Sacred Scripture is bolstered and given a divine guarantee through the miracles of Christ, most importantly his resurrection from the dead. We read in Vatican II's *Dei Verbum*, the Dogmatic Constitution on Divine Revelation:

> To see Jesus is to see His Father (John 14:9). For this reason Jesus perfected revelation by fulfilling it through His whole work of making Himself present and manifesting Himself: through His words and deeds, His signs and wonders, but especially through His death and glorious resurrection from the dead and final sending of the Spirit of truth. Moreover He confirmed with divine testimony what revelation proclaimed, that God is with us to free us from the darkness of sin and death, and to raise us up to life eternal. (no. 4)

The miracles of Christ and the subsequent works of the apostles in his name come down to us through Sacred Scripture, which is considered to be *public* revelation, as it is valid for all time and meant for all. Miracles and messages received after the death of the last evangelist, John — even extensively studied and Church-authorized spiritual insights given to history's greatest saints — are considered *private* revelation. In his *Message of Fatima*, Joseph Cardinal Ratzinger (the future Benedict XVI) reminded Catholics of the importance of public revelation (as opposed to private revelation) found in Scripture:

> The term "public Revelation" refers to the revealing action of God directed to humanity as a whole and which finds its literary expression in the two parts of the Bible: the Old and New Testaments.... It is valid for all time, and it has reached its fulfillment in the life, death, and resurrection of Jesus Christ. In Christ, God has said everything, that is, he has revealed himself completely, and therefore revelation came to an end with the fulfillment of the mystery of Christ as enunciated in the New Testament.[7]

In his apostolic exhortation *Verbum Domini*, he speaks of the unique value of private revelation:

> The value of private revelations is essentially different from that of the one public revelation: the latter demands faith.... Private revelation is an aid to this faith, and it demonstrates its credibility precisely because it refers back to the one public revelation.... A private revelation can introduce new emphases, give rise to new forms of piety, or deepen older ones. It can have a certain prophetic character and can be a valuable aid for better understanding and living the Gospel at a certain time; consequently it should not be treated lightly. It is a help which is proffered, but its use is not obligatory.[8]

The dogmatic constitution *Dei Filius* from Vatican I reminds us that miracles are external signs provided by God as arguments on behalf of revelation.[9] The *Catechism of the Catholic Church* (CCC), in paragraph 156, thus relates this expression of the purpose of miracles:

> So "that the submission of our faith might nevertheless be in accordance with reason, God willed that external proofs of his Revelation should be joined to the internal helps of the Holy Spirit" (*Dei Filius* 3: DS 3009). Thus the miracles of Christ and the saints, prophecies, the Church's growth and holiness, and her fruitfulness and stability "are the most certain signs of divine Revelation, adapted to the intelligence of all"; they are "motives of credibility" (*motiva credibilitatis*), which show that the assent of faith is "by no means a blind impulse of the mind" (*Dei Filius* 3008–3010; cf. Mk 16 20; Heb 2:4).

To deny the existence or the possibility of miracles is an error that would put a person outside of communion with the Church (anathema):

> If anyone shall say that miracles are impossible, and therefore that all the accounts regarding them, even those contained in Holy Scripture, are to be dismissed as fables or myths; or that miracles can never be known with certainty, and that the divine origin of Christianity cannot be proved by them; let him be anathema.[10]

For all the caution that is necessary to relegate miraculous phenomena to their proper role as supports that lead the faithful to Christ, it would be a mistake to underestimate the importance of miracles in the life and history of the Church. Catholic philosopher Dietrich von Hildebrand (1889–1977) reminds us:

> One of the great purposes of Vatican II was to enliven the religious life of the faithful. True enlivenment requires that the supernatural spirit of Christ be fully thrown into relief. That means eliminating any blurring of the distinction between the natural and supernatural.[11]

Throughout the Old Testament we hear stories of God's intervention to protect his chosen people. There are stories of divine favor for great saints such as Joan of Arc, who received inspired messages and protection in battle. In the famous Battle of Lepanto in 1571, Christian forces overcame great odds and the formidable Turkish fleet with all of Europe praying the Rosary and General Andrea Doria sailing with a copy of the miraculous image of Our Lady of Guadalupe in his ship's stateroom. In a few select Marian apparition accounts, Our Lady has come to the aid of those in need in time of war. In April 1900, local accounts report that when the Boxer Rebellion broke out in China, ten thousand hostile soldiers attacked the small, impoverished mission village of Dong Lu, home to a thousand Christians. The Virgin Mary appeared in the sky as a beautiful lady in white, surrounded by light. The soldiers, in a senseless rage, started to shoot into the sky. Then the attackers suddenly fled, frightened, when a fiery horseman — perhaps St. Michael — chased them out of the village, and they never returned. As recently as 2009, Russians and Georgians reported a miraculous apparition of the Virgin in the sky during military actions in South Ossetia that ended the battle.[12]

The Faith has not only been protected by miracles but has grown as a result of them as well. Many conversions can be traced to the influence of the supernatural and in fact are some of the spiritual fruits that are assessed in declaring phenomena worthy of belief. Nine million baptisms in Mexico City alone in the seven or eight years following the events in Guadalupe in 1531 speak to this important role, as accounted by Franciscan priest and early historian of New Spain Toribio de Benavente Motolinia in 1541.

Countless stories of conversions involving the Miraculous Medal given to St. Catherine Labouré in a vision on November 27, 1830, attest to this as well. In perhaps the most famous account from 1842, Marie Alphonse Ratisbonne, an anti-Catholic Jew, befriended a baron in Rome and began wearing a Miraculous Medal as a simple test. While waiting for his friend in the church Sant'Andrea delle Fratte, Ratisbonne saw a vision of the Blessed Virgin Mary. He then quickly converted to Catholicism, joined the priesthood, and began a ministry for the conversion of Jews.

Another prime example, this one without Church approval, occurred in 1944 in Mississippi, when Claude Newman was imprisoned for a shooting and was sentenced to death. Given a Miraculous Medal to wear by his cellmate, he later had a glowing vision of the Blessed Virgin Mary, who advised him to summon a priest. His conversion quickly followed, and the night before his execution, he celebrated with other prisoners as he awaited his eternal reward.

The spiritual fruits of a miracle can take a more concrete form. Some of the largest churches in the world, for example, are built as a result of holy visions. Four of the twelve largest church buildings in the world (by square footage) have their origins in appearances of the Mother of God: the Basilica of Our Lady of Good Health in India, the Basilica of Our Lady of Guadalupe in Mexico City, Nuestra Señora de la Aparecida in Brazil, and Santa Maria Maggiore in Rome. One of the great churches of Rome, Santa Maria Maggiore was built after an apparition of Our Lady of the Snows in 358, according to pious tradition. Legend says that she appeared to both Pope Liberius and a wealthy childless couple who then donated the money for construction after seeing a floor plan of the future church outlined in snow on a hill. Although Pope Sixtus III[13] did not include the story when he rededicated the basilica a few centuries later and the reference to the legend (and the title Sanctae Mariae ad Nives, "Our Lady of the Snows") was removed in the 1969 revision of the General Roman Calendar,[14] the faithful still honor the miraculous story when, during the memorial feast day, white rose petals are dropped in a snow-like shower from the dome of the Chapel of Our Lady.

The fact that the church of Santa Maria Maggiore resulted from a vision is far from unique. A great number of the 2,500 reported Marian apparitions throughout history have involved the request that a chapel, a church, or a sanctuary be built in Our Lady's honor. In "the Great Event" of the apparitions in Guadalupe in 1531, according to the earliest account, the *Nican Mopohua*, Our Lady asks St. Juan Diego:

> I wish that a temple be erected here quickly, so I may therein exhibit and give all my love, compassion, help, and protection, because I am your merciful mother, to you, and to all the inhabitants on this land and all the rest who love me, invoke and confide in me; listen there to their lamentations; and remedy all their miseries, afflictions and sorrows.

Some of the other apparition events around the world that gave inspiration to the building of shrines are worthy of belief, and others are legends that sprung up later. Still other origin stories are based on oral tradition and were put into writing at a much later date.

For example, one of the great pilgrimage sites in Spain, Our Lady of the Pillar in Zaragoza, originating in a miracle and housing an ancient jasper Marian image on a column, did not always recognize Our Lady under this title. According to the legend relating to the apostle St. James the Greater and his travels in Spain, on January 2 in the year 40, he was disheartened with his lack of success in proclaiming the gospel in Caesaraugusta (present-day Zaragoza) by the river Ebro, when he saw Mary (still alive at the time) miraculously appear on a pillar, comforting him and calling him to return to Jerusalem. The first written mention of the Virgin of Zaragoza comes from a bishop in the middle of the twelfth century, and Zaragoza's co-cathedral's name did not originally include a reference to El Pilar, being called Santa Maria Mayor. In 1296, Pope Boniface VIII conferred an indulgence on pilgrims visiting this shrine but still without mention of Our Lady of the Pillar. One of the legal councils of Zaragoza first wrote about Our Lady under this title in 1299, promising safety and privileges to pilgrims who came to visit the shrine. In 1456, Pope Calixtus III issued a bull encouraging pilgrimage to Our Lady of the Pillar and confirming the name and the miraculous origin. So, despite the lack of early extant texts about the miracle story and the name of this devotion, the enduring tradition delivers the story to us today.

One of the greatest miracle stories in the history of the Catholic Church comes from the tradition surrounding a shrine itself being legendarily miraculous. The Holy House of Loreto (*Santa Casa di Loreto*) is reputed to be the actual former home of the Virgin Mary. The legend recounts that in 1291, when the house was threatened by Muslims, it was carried by angels through the air and deposited in Trsat, a suburb of Rijeka, Croatia. Later, in 1294, angels carried it again across the Adriatic Sea to Loreto. Since the fourteenth century, this small house, surrounded by the Basilica della Santa Casa, has been a major place of pilgrimage — visited by many saints and popes — and healing miracles.

Many of these apparition-based churches play a major role in the lives of the faithful around the world. They serve as some of the most frequented destinations for pilgrimages. Each year ten million people go to Mexico City to venerate the miraculous tilma of Our Lady of Guadalupe, five million visit Lourdes in France, and four million make the trip to Fátima, Portugal. Since 1981, more than thirty million pilgrims have gone to the alleged apparition site of Medjugorje in Bosnia-Herzegovina. Such numbers seem to indicate that the miraculous continues to play an active role in the life of the Church.

The Faith has grown and developed throughout the ages with the influence of the supernatural. Miracles have helped foster an increase in devotions as well as the spread and acceptance of specific Marian dogmas (e.g., the Immaculate Conception in the case of Lourdes). Many devotions and devotionals claim supernatural origins by virtue of referencing an originating Marian apparition. The Rosary is legendarily attributed to an apparition to St. Dominic in 1208, and St. Simon Stock is said to have received the first brown scapular from Our Lady in 1251 in Aylesford, England. Other colors of scapulars have their own legendarily miraculous beginnings. The most popular Catholic medal in circulation continues to be the Miraculous Medal, whose divine design was conferred during the apparitions received by St. Catherine Labouré in Rue du Bac, France, in 1830. Also according to legend, the creation of the popular St. Michael Prayer is attributed to Pope Leo XIII's response to a vision he experienced in which the Lord gave permission to the devil to do what he wanted to humanity during the twentieth century. While the troubles around the world in that century seem to support such an occurrence, the documentation surrounding it is in fact lacking.

Most of us do not find ourselves surrounded by the great miracles recounted to us from an earlier age. The saints provide an excellent example of how to follow Christ in our ordinary, everyday lives, but many displayed some mystical gifts that appear far from ordinary, whether it was seeing visions or bearing the wounds of Christ. The Council of Trent (1545–1563) relates the importance of the miracles of the saints:

Through God's saints miracles and salutary examples are put before our eyes that we might imitate the life and customs of the saints and be stirred up to love God and foster piety.[15]

In addition to honoring these miracle-working saints on feasts throughout the year, we celebrate our Church's great moments of divine intervention throughout the Roman Calendar with commemorations for Divine Mercy, Our Lady of Lourdes, Our Lady of Mount Carmel, Our Lady of Fátima, and Our Lady of Guadalupe.

The role of miracles has extended beyond impacting the devotional life of the lay faithful. A number of religious orders have their roots in divine inspiration received by their founders. On August 1, 1218, the Virgin Mary, later honored under the title of Our Lady of Ransom (or Our Lady of Mercy), is said to have appeared to St. Peter Nolasco, to his confessor, St. Raymund of Pennafort, and to King James of Aragon and through these three men established a work for the redemption of captives. She desired the establishment of the Mercedarian religious order (whose name derives from the Spanish word *merced*, "mercy"). Its members seek to free Christian captives and offer themselves, if necessary, as an exchange.

Less than two decades later, seven men of the Florentine nobility were involved in the brotherhood of "Laude" to venerate the Holy Virgin Mary. On the feast of the Assumption, the Blessed Virgin appeared to them to urge them to make their lives even holier and more perfect. They decided to follow her advice and left the business world to retire to a life of prayer and penance, especially giving themselves over to the veneration of the Virgin Mary. On Good Friday in 1239, Mary appeared again and showed them a black cassock that they should wear when they established a new religious order. The order would spread especially the veneration of the Sorrows that the Blessed Virgin experienced during Christ's Passion and Crucifixion. Thus arose the Order of the Servants of Mary, more commonly known as the Servites, who found rapid and wide dissemination. The seven founders of the Order of the Servants were all canonized.

Other orders derived from a vision include the Passionists (St. Paul of the Cross, 1720), the Sisterhood of Our Lady of Sion (Alphonse Ratisbonne, 1842), and the Sisters of the Rosary (Bl. Mother Marie-Alphonsine Ghattas, 1880). All these orders were founded at the request of the Virgin. Even Opus Dei, a personal prelature within the Church, was founded in 1928 by St. Josemaría Escríva after he claimed a supernatural vision of this work.

Throughout the Church's history, miracle stories have been woven into the fabric of Catholic tradition and have played a significant role in the lives of the faithful. The insights and inspirations provided in miraculous events and messages have come in times of great crisis for individuals, nations, and the universal Church.

CHAPTER 2

What Should We Do
with Miracles?

The question of the role of miracles in our life of faith is an important one and requires avoiding two extremes: an overemphasis and credulity regarding the supernatural on the one hand and a denial of the possibility of divine intervention and a diminishment of the role of popular devotion on the other. Sometimes it is hard to discern the amount of emphasis we should place on what St. John XXIII called "those supernatural lights."

Excessive, obsessive expression of belief by the faithful in miraculous phenomena is not only the reason the Church is methodical and cautious in approving any occurrence as authentic but also a primary impetus for performing any investigations in the first place. The unspoken goal of such examination is to prove that nothing supernatural is occurring at these places, in order that the faithful might return to a more authentic and grounded practice of their faith. But because there is typically such a tremendous swell of support and interest surrounding a purported miraculous event, the Church by necessity *must* investigate and provide pastoral guidance on the matter.

Although seeking miracles is often an attempt to quench an authentic thirst for the spiritual and an opportunity to quell spiritual doubts, miraculous phenomena are not a substitute for absolute faith in God. The center of the Catholic Faith can be found in the person, acts, and words of Jesus Christ. A great demonstration of true faith comes in a story about St. Louis (King Louis IX of France from 1226 to 1270). While St. Louis was working in his study, a courier came running in to inform him of a miracle happening at that very moment: an image of the infant Jesus appeared on the host during Eucharistic adoration. The saintly king calmly continued his writing and quietly responded: "I could not believe more firmly in Christ's presence in the Eucharist if I were to behold a miracle."[16]

Private revelation can serve as the special insights of saints who received messages from the Blessed Mother. The content of such messages does not belong to the deposit of faith, and as such, belief in approved private revelations — even in the most highly recognized and celebrated miraculous events like Fátima and Lourdes — is never required by faith. Joseph Cardinal Ratzinger, when he was prefect of the Congregation for the Doctrine of the Faith (CDF), the Vatican body with the final word on miracle claims, acknowledged this fact but warned against ignoring the signs given to us by God:

> No apparition is indispensable to the faith.... But we certainly cannot prevent God from speaking to our time through the simple persons and also through extraordinary signs that point to the insufficiency of cultures stamped by rationalism that dominate us.[17]

The Church is clear about the role of private revelations but devotes a mere eight lines to the topic in its official compilation of doctrine for the faithful, the *Cathechism of the Catholic Church*. The *Catechism* states:

> Throughout the ages, there have been so-called "private" revelations, some of which have been recognized by the

authority of the Church. They do not belong, however, to the deposit of faith. It is not their role to improve or complete Christ's definitive Revelation, but to help live more fully by it in a certain period of history. Guided by the magisterium of the Church, the *sensus fidelium* knows how to discern and welcome in these revelations whatever constitutes an authentic call of Christ or his saints to the Church. (CCC 67)

It is not uncommon for believers to be swept up in chasing the latest miracle or alleged message from the heavens. Caught up in a sort of modern Gnosticism — the seeking of *gnosis*, or secret knowledge — people hunger for any hidden information they can garner about the return of Christ. This often results in end-times fanaticism or an apocalyptic view of current world events. Therefore, Cardinal Ratzinger reminded the faithful about private revelation — and Marian apparitions in particular — and its primary Christocentric purpose:

To all curious people, I would say I am certain that the Virgin does not engage in sensationalism; she does not act in order to instigate fear. She does not present apocalyptic visions, but guides people to her Son. And this is what is essential. The Madonna did not appear to children, to the small, to the simple, to those unknown in the world in order to create a sensation. Mary's purpose is, through these simple ones, to call the world back to simplicity, that is, to the essentials: conversion, prayer, and the sacraments.[18]

Without full knowledge of all the facts surrounding alleged phenomena, it is important for the faithful to rely on the judgments of the competent ecclesial authority — the local bishop — in providing pastoral guidance on these matters. The bishop safeguards his flock from being exposed to theologically unsound private revelation or other dangers related to the pursuit of alleged phenomena. The University of Dayton's International Marian Research Institute identifies the requisite obedience of Catholics to the discernment of the local bishop as dictated by canon law:

> As the bishops are entrusted with the responsibilities of discerning and ruling on apparitions as stemming from the nature of their office, so there are fundamental responsibilities on the part of the members of the diocese. First, they are to obey their bishops when the episcopate acts as Christ's representatives (canon 212), that is, when they teach formally or establish binding discipline as pastors of a particular church. This obedience owed to the bishops in their capacity as leaders of particular churches is intended to promote the common good. Canon 753 also speaks of the "religious assent" owed to the bishops' teaching authority, which means a special quality of respect and gratitude, along with critical awareness and good will. Therefore, there should be intelligent obedience to ecclesiastical authority in the matter of alleged apparitions.[19]

Not only must the faithful follow the guidance of the bishop on these delicate matters, but also, more importantly, the alleged mystic and his corresponding organizations must be open to the guidance of authority. Sometimes the process is imperfect, considering that a local bishop might be personally biased against a certain miraculous claim or might want to limit the distraction that such phenomena can bring. A sensible rule of thumb might be: "A superior may or may not be inspired by God in his command, but you are always inspired in obeying."[20]

In many of the cases of phenomena rejected by Church authorities, disobedience has been prevalent. One ongoing example is Maureen Sweeney-Kyle, who began to claim visions in 1996 and created the "Holy Love" movement in Elyria, Ohio. After various warnings and guidance, Richard Lennon, Bishop of Cleveland, on November 11, 2009, issued a decree declaring the events not supernatural, forbidding the participation of priests and laity in those events, and prohibiting the organization from calling itself Catholic. Despite the statement, Holy Love still continues under ecumenical auspices. Likewise, the initially promising apparitions claimed by Mary Ann Van Hoof in the 1950s in Necedah, Wisconsin, were condemned due to many factors, including the disobedience of the visionary. An enormous shrine was later erected and still exists today as part of an Old Catholic sect.

Conversely, authentic mystics have shown obedience at times of great difficulty. In his September 1, 2010, General Audience, Pope Benedict lauded the obedience of St. Hildegard von Bingen, who later became one of the Doctors of the Church:

As always happens in the life of true mystics, Hildegard too wanted to put herself under the authority of wise people to discern the origin of her visions, fearing that they were the product of illusions and did not come from God.... This is the seal of an authentic experience of the Holy Spirit, the source of every charism: The person endowed with supernatural gifts never boasts of them, never flaunts them and, above all, shows complete obedience to the ecclesial authority.

The widely practiced and well-known devotion to the Sacred Heart of Jesus stems from the revelations of Jesus to the French nun St. Margaret Mary Alacoque in a series of apparitions from 1673 to 1675. On one occasion, Jesus told St. Margaret Mary to do something, but her superior did not approve it. Jesus reminded her:

> Not only do I desire that you should do what your superior commands, but also that you should do nothing of all that I order without their consent. I love obedience, and without it no one can please me.[21]

And later Our Lord told her:

> Listen, My daughter, and do not lightly believe and trust every spirit, for Satan is angry and will try to deceive you. So do nothing without the approval of those who guide you. Being thus under the authority of obedience, his efforts against you will be in vain, for he has no power over the obedient.[22]

Obedience played an important role in perhaps the most famous instance of the Church's changing its stance on the assessment of private revelation — the universally approved and widely celebrated Divine Mercy devotion, originating in visions of Christ and the Virgin Mary as received by Polish nun St. Faustina Kowalska (1905–1938). Initially prohibitions were placed on the messages of the apparitions by the local bishop and the Congregation for the Doctrine of the Faith. This condemnation was finally lifted in 1978 through the work of St. John Paul II, who later not only canonized St. Faustina but also established a feast on the General Roman Calendar. Celebrated on the Sunday after

Easter, the feast day includes specific indulgences that are granted under the usual conditions. These great honors and devotions occurred only after many years of obediently ceasing public celebration or distribution of the message found in Faustina's *Diary*. St. Faustina wrote about the challenges of pride: "Satan can even clothe himself in a cloak of humility, but he does not know how to wear the cloak of obedience" (*Diary*, par. 939).

St. Padre Pio, the famous Capuchin friar from Pietrelcina, is another exemplary model of obedience. Because of the need to investigate his tremendous mystical gifts, reportedly including the stigmata, bilocation, and the ability to read souls, and because of the public curiosity surrounding those gifts, Church authorities suppressed his ability to say Mass publicly. St. Pio was obedient until his death in 1968 and was canonized in 2002.

For all the many instances of inauthentic or invalid devotions and miracle claims being shut down, throughout history in countries around the world, Church authorities have validated hundreds and even thousands of reports of miraculous events. The majority of the occurrences that have any level of ecclesiastical sanction enjoy a traditional mode of approval. That is, if they occurred in the era prior to the Council of Trent (1545–1563), their approval typically was rooted in enduring tradition resulting from popular acclaim and a strong *sensus fidelium*, or universal acknowledgment from the faithful. It wasn't until the beginning of the seventeenth century that miracle claims were more rigorously investigated and began to rely on science in addition to the prayerful discernment that had marked investigations of the past. In establishing an event as having supernatural character and being worthy of belief, the bishops and their investigative commissions hope to use scientific inquiry and modern technology to arrive at these difficult decisions with moral certitude that the alleged miracle cannot be attributable to natural causes or human delusion. But even if science cannot offer explanations about the phenomena that often purported divine messages, Christian faith cannot accept "revelations" that claim to surpass or correct the revelation of which Christ is the fulfillment, as is the case in certain non-Christian religions and also in certain recent sects that base themselves on such "revelations."

CHAPTER 3

Miracle or Fraud? —
How the Church Decides

Not everything is in fact a miracle. Quite popular are claims of an image of Jesus, the Blessed Virgin Mary, or the saints seen in a light, a shadow, or a discoloration. The most infamous example is the 2004 sale for $10,000 of a grilled-cheese sandwich that bore the likeness of the Virgin Mary. Science classifies such imagery as a form of pareidolia, a false perception of an image due to what is theorized as the mind's oversensitivity to perceiving patterns. Whereas the image of Our Lady of Guadalupe miraculously "painted" on the tilma of St. Juan Diego in 1531 on Tepeyac Hill in Mexico is perhaps the greatest prodigy in the history of the Church after the time of the Gospels, there is only one instance of a naturally occurring stain resembling the Virgin Mary that has ever been approved by ecclesiastical authorities. On January 17, 1797, in Absam, Austria, a permanent image inexplicably impressed on a glass window was declared miraculous by the local bishop.

An instance of a bleeding host or statue needs to be treated with a different level of attention and intervention than a case of a person who allegedly bleeds from the wounds of Christ. In the case of the Eucharistic miracle, the host is typically confiscated by Church authorities to perform scientific tests that can easily ferret out a hoax from an authentic miracle. In some rare cases, actual human blood or heart muscle has been found to be present with the host.

In cases of the stigmata, by which a person is allegedly joined in suffering with the crucified Christ, blood oozes from the person's hands, feet, side, and forehead. These persons are kept under close medical observation to see the spontaneity of the bleeding and to ensure that the persons are not self-inflicting the wounds with sharp implements or acid. If there is no scientific explanation for a person's stigmata, the Church will not publicly declare the authenticity of the occurrence, as it is tantamount to the canonization of a living person in the eyes of some of the faithful. Some of the Church's greatest saints, such as Francis of Assisi and Catherine of Siena, have been stigmatics, but the wounds themselves are not a guarantee of holiness.

Those who bear the wounds of Christ are still subject to the same temptations and failings as the rest of us, but when a stigmatic publicly falters, there is the potential for great scandal. One of Catholicism's great modern saints, Padre Pio of Pietrelcina, as mentioned in the last chapter, exhibited these wounds but was censured by the Vatican and prohibited from publicly saying Mass in order to allow Church authorities to assess the many miracles and phenomena that surrounded him.

In the case of incorruptible bodies that are preserved in some state of perfection well beyond the time of death, the former Sacred Congregation of Rites had given official recognition to several preservations as miraculous. In general the Church has been reluctant to use the incorruption of a body as a miracle in a sainthood cause, with the notable exception of St. Andrew Bobola, whose corpse survived rough handling during several translations and still remained perfectly fresh for more than three hundred years.[23]

The Vatican is generally very cautious and can be extremely slow to approve miracles of any sort. For example, in 2008 the

Church finally gave formal recognition to the 1664 apparitions in Le Laus, France, and the first formal approval of an apparition in the United States came in 2010, when the visions experienced by Belgian farmworker Adele Brise in 1859 in Wisconsin were solemnly approved. In the 1947 case of Bruno Cornacchiola, a poor Italian tram worker who received a vision of the Blessed Virgin Mary on his way to assassinate the pope, the Vicariate of Rome approved the cult of the Virgin of Revelation very quickly that same year, but a definitive judgment, either positive or negative in regard to the supernaturality of the vision, has still not been made. With modern communication technologies, more advanced record keeping, and a wider geographical impact of claims of private revelation resulting in larger pastoral concerns, the Church has moved more swiftly in recent times.

In the early Church, there were no scientific inquiries into the events in question. Not only were there no brain-wave monitors or video cameras to track eye movement during supposed visions or tests to determine whether the blood or tears on a weeping statue were human, no formal investigation of any sort was universally required in the discernment of the miraculous claims. As part of the process, the faithful might gather to pray at the site, and the parish priest, or even better, a bishop could be involved, but it wasn't the norm. Trustworthy testimony and a miracle were typically the main elements that built a case for visions or other events to be accepted as authentic. In a form of popular approval throughout Europe, shrines arose, including the Slipper Chapel in Walsingham, England, where Catholics and Anglicans alike commemorate the apparitions experienced by a noblewoman in 1061, and, as was mentioned earlier, Our Lady of the Pilar Basilica in Spain, legendarily the site of history's first Marian apparition experienced by St. James in A.D. 40 while Mary was still alive.

It is not uncommon in early stories of miraculous visions or holy images for a formula to be present in one of several variations: Our Lady appears to one or more people (or a miraculous statue is discovered), she requests that the visionary tells the town to return to a life of practicing the Faith, a miracle (most typically healing) is given to prove the authenticity of the Virgin's presence, and finally she requests that a shrine be built in commemoration. The location of the requested shrine is often indicated symbolically — the collected statue might miraculously return overnight three times to the spot where it was discovered. This was the case in the foundational legend of the Santuario de Chimayó in New Mexico, known as the Lourdes of the Southwest and home to the healing dirt that has been a part of thousands of cures. The location for the shrine was chosen because a supernatural light was said to have shone on a crucifix that was unearthed and taken to the local parish church some miles away. Three times it miraculously returned to its original discovery spot, giving the faithful confidence to build a shrine there.

In other such legends, the image became so heavy that it could not be moved. In the year 641, villagers of Soviore, Italy, buried their statue of the Madonna and fled toward the Mediterranean escaping the advancing Lombard hordes. A hundred years later, on July 7, 740, the parish priest was hunting at dawn, when he noticed a dove fly into a hole. Unsuccessful at uncovering the spot, he returned the next day with three helpers with shovels, and they unearthed a wooden statue. When the priest tried to carry it home, it was too heavy to move, so he left it there. On the following day, people found that the statue had moved to the top of a nearby chestnut tree. When it repeatedly returned after being moved, the villagers built a chapel at that spot.

The most famous legend of a weight-gaining holy icon is that of the wonder-working Polish image of Our Lady of

Czestochowa. Hussite raiders looted the castle where the icon was housed, but during the getaway the image became so heavy that the horses could no longer drag the cart carrying the goods. The thieves removed the image and slashed it with a sword in frustration before tossing the icon into a ravine. The iconic scar present in every reproduction of the Black Madonna of Jasna Gora faithfully reproduces the scar on the face of the original image. Eventually, however, miracles and revelations perhaps intended for the universal Church were no longer evaluated by a parish priest or a community of the faithful, and more standard guidelines were drawn up. The revelations accorded to mystic St. Birgitta (Bridget) of Sweden were considered at the Councils of Constance (1414–1418) and Basel (1431–1449). She had received in ecstasy hundreds of infused locutions relating to a wide range of topics, including tips for everyday living, calls for reform in the Church and in Sweden, and even the Crusades. She dictated her messages in Swedish to two spiritual directors and a bishop, who recorded them in Latin. Because of her high profile and contact with the popes on political matters, her revelations were treated with special care and attention.[24]

The proliferation of alleged messages from myriad seers inspired greater Church involvement in discerning the words of mystics. Toward the end of the fifteenth century, the faithful were growing anxious over the increase in itinerant prophets with messages of doom.[25] The Fifth Lateran Council (1512–1517), called by Pope Julius, reserved the approval of new prophecies and revelations to the Holy See. Following the explosive and scandalous exposing as a demonic fraud the famed Spanish mystic Sr. Magdalena de la Cruz in 1544, the Council of Trent sought to return investigations to the local level and authorized bishops to investigate and approve such phenomena before public worship could take place.

As established in the Council of Trent, the local bishop is the first and main authority in apparition cases, which can be defined as instances of private revelation. From the twenty-fifth session of the Council of Trent:

And that these things may be the more faithfully observed, the holy Synod ordains, that no one be allowed to place, or cause to be placed, any unusual image, in any place, or church, howsoever exempted, except that image have been approved of by the bishop: also, that no new miracles are to be acknowledged, or new relics recognized, unless the said bishop has taken cognizance and approved thereof; who, as soon as he has obtained some certain information in regard to these matters, shall, after having taken the advice of theologians, and of other pious men, act therein as he shall judge to be consonant with truth and piety. But if any doubtful, or difficult abuse has to be extirpated; or, in fine, if any more grave question shall arise touching these matters, the bishop, before deciding the controversy, shall await the sentence of the metropolitan and of the bishops of the province, in a provincial Council; yet so, that nothing new, or that previously has not been usual in the Church, shall be resolved on, without having first consulted the most holy Roman Pontiff.[26]

In the decades following the council, the Church became increasingly vigilant about protecting the faithful against alleged private revelation and, in general, against the expression of ideas deemed dangerous. With the development and popularity of the printing press, many anti-Catholic documents and reformed versions of the Bible became widely available. The Catholic Church sought to protect the faithful from publications deemed heretical, anti-clerical, or lascivious and created a list known as the Index of Forbidden Books (*Index Librorum Prohibitorum*) in 1559. In addition to books deemed dangerous in science and philosophy, writings on unapproved private revelation would make the list. In 1588, Pope Sixtus V established the Roman Inquisition (also known as the Supreme Sacred Congregation of the Roman and Universal Inquisition) and fourteen other congregations in the Roman Curia.

Prospero Lambertini (1675–1758), the future Benedict XIV, provided several rules for discernment of private revelations and the miracles needed for the canonization of saints in *De Servorum Dei Beatificatione et Beatorum Canonizatione* in 1740. Such events must present themselves to human reason as being truly extraordinary and beyond the scope of natural causes. He answered the question of whether the incorruptible corpses of saints could be used as evidence of sainthood, insisting that the cases considered miraculous had to be bodies close to perfectly preserved over the course of many years.[27]

In the twentieth century, the Church continued its efforts to contain the wide dissemination of information on alleged phenomena and reinforced the bishop's role as judge of the authenticity of private revelation. The Code of Canon Law of 1917 (canon 1399, no. 5) forbade the publication of anything about "new apparitions, revelations, visions, prophecies, and miracles" without the local bishop's approbation. The local ordinary is to consult someone (known as the *censor librorum*) whom he considers competent to give the doctrinal content of the publication the stamp of *nihil obstat* ("nothing forbids"), at which point the local ordinary grants the mark of *imprimatur* ("let it be printed").

On December 7, 1965, following Pope Paul VI's motu proprio *Integrae servandae* reconstituting the Holy Office as the Sacred Congregation for the Doctrine of the Faith (CDF) and effectively dropping the Index of Forbidden Books from being overseen by any congregation, a CDF notification of June 14, 1966, published in the Vatican's newspaper, *L'Osservatore Romano*,[28] announced that, while the Index maintained its moral force in teaching Christians to avoid those writings that could endanger faith and morals, it no longer had the force of Church law and its repercussions.

In 1966, Paul VI, implementing Vatican II's statement on the right of the mass media to information, lifted the requirement that all writings about private revelation need ecclesiastical approval before publication, repealing canons 1399 and 2318 from the Code of Canon Law of 1917. With this change and the disappearance of the Index, the floodgates for claims of private revelation had been opened. Fr. René Laurentin, the world's foremost Mariologist, acknowledged the change in apparition trends by labeling the rise "an explosion of the supernatural" and expressed concern that the reports of apparitions had become frequent, "numerous and even disturbing."[29] He found this to be such a paradigm shift that he divided the almost 2,500 apparitions catalogued in his comprehensive work, *Dictionary of the Apparitions of the Virgin Mary*, into two parts: (1) apparitions in Christian history before 1966 and (2) those occurring after.

The most recent CDF document and the current standard that lays out the guidelines for the judgment of apparition claims is the *Normae Congregationis de Modo Procedendi in Diudicandis Praesumptis Apparitionibus ac Revelationibus* (*Norms of the Congregation for Proceeding in Judging Alleged Apparitions and Revelations*), approved by Pope Paul VI on February 27, 1978, and written *sub secreto* in Latin for the eyes of bishops alone. The document was later publicly produced in translations released to the bishops. With these official translations having been leaked to the

Internet and other unofficial translations abounding online, the Vatican formally released five translations of the document more than two decades later on May 24, 2012, admitting knowledge of its previous availability in the introduction by William Cardinal Levada.[30] The purpose of the document, as indicated by Levada in his introduction, is to

> aid the Pastors of the Catholic Church in their difficult task of discerning presumed apparitions, revelations, messages or, more generally, extraordinary phenomena of presumed supernatural origin.... [May it also] be useful to theologians and experts in this field of the lived experience of the Church, whose delicacy requires an ever-more thorough consideration.

The *Normae Congregationis* sets out the procedures to be followed in investigating the authenticity of extraordinary claims. The document clarifies the role of Church officials in investigating the authenticity of claims of private revelation. There are four ways the competent ecclesiastical authority is to act with respect to a claim of private revelation. The authority can or must:

1. Inform himself without delay and keep vigilance over the claim.
2. Promote some form of cult/devotion at the request of the faithful if the above negative and positive criteria do not prohibit it.
3. Intervene on his own initiative, especially in grave circumstances.
4. Refrain from intervening in doubtful cases, but remain vigilant.

Bishops evaluate evidence of private revelation according to these guidelines:

1. The facts in the case are free of error.
2. The person(s) receiving the messages is/are psychologically balanced, honest, moral, sincere, and respectful of Church authority.
3. Doctrinal errors are not attributed to God, the Virgin Mary, or to a saint.
4. Theological and spiritual doctrines presented are free of error.
5. Moneymaking is not a motive involved in the events.
6. Healthy religious devotion and spiritual fruits result, with no evidence of collective hysteria.

St. Philip Neri (1515–1595) was often brought in by bishops to give his opinion on the authenticity of mystics. With a careful eye on obedience and humility, he was able to ferret out false mystics with great success. One day in 1560, the cardinals were discerning about a nun who was having visions. Since they sought his opinion, Philip went to see the young sister. He kindly said to her, "Sister, I didn't want to see you; I wanted to see the saint." The nun answered, "But I am the saint!" and Philip was able to report confidently to the cardinals that her visions were not from God.[31]

Judgment can find that a revelation shows all the signs of being an authentic supernatural intervention from heaven, that it is clearly not miraculous, or that there are not sufficient signs to establish whether the alleged apparition is authentic.

If a vision of the Virgin Mary, for example, is recognized by the bishop, it means that the associated message is not contrary to faith and morals and that Mary can be venerated in a special way at the site. Pope Benedict XVI commented on private revelation in his 2010 apostolic exhortation *Verbum Domini*:

Ecclesiastical approval of a private revelation essentially means that its message contains nothing contrary to faith and morals. It is licit to make it public and the faithful are authorized to give to it their prudent adhesion. A private revelation can introduce new emphases, give rise to new forms of piety, or deepen older ones. It can have a certain prophetic character (cf. *1 Th* 5:19–21) and can be a valuable aid for better understanding and living the Gospel at a certain time; consequently it should not be treated lightly. It is a help which is proffered, but its use is not obligatory. (no. 14)

According to Tradition, the "competent authority" refers to the local ordinary, who is expected to fulfill the duties and obligations that fall to him. Although the diocesan bishop possesses the right to initiate an investigation, that country's national conference of bishops can subsequently intervene at his request or at the request of a qualified group of faithful not "motivated by suspect reasons." If necessary, the Vatican can then also intervene if the situation involves the Church at large or if discernment requires it. The CDF judges the manner in which the local ordinary conducted his investigation and decides whether it is necessary to initiate a new examination. It is the right and responsibility of local bishops to investigate and make judgments about alleged apparitions, and ordinarily the Vatican does not become involved in the process. The Congregation for the Doctrine of the Faith has an obligation of "guidance and vigilance."

In an essay for *Pontificia Academia Mariana Internationalis (PAMI)* on the topic of *Normae Congregationis*, Msgr. Charles Scicluna, promoter of justice for the Congregation for the Doctrine of the Faith, notes that once a decision of the CDF is given, it cannot be overturned by a lower authority, as it is of "undisputed hierarchical authority."[32]

A classic modern example of the progression in the levels of intervening authority is the controversial Medjugorje case, in which the famed apparition phenomenon that began in 1981 was first investigated and discouraged by the local ordinary, was later judged to be "not established as supernatural" by the 1991 Zadar Commission of the Yugoslavian bishops, and then was re-examined by a Vatican commission formed on March 26, 2010. (Note: At the time of the publication of this book, the results of the commission were unknown.)

Church officials are called to assess the phenomenon and the people who report them, looking for evidence of authenticity. Typically, if the situation merits it, the bishop will assemble a commission of experts in various disciplines to create a report to advise him on how to render judgment. These experts may come from a variety of fields and are usually theologians, psychologists, psychiatrists, Mariologists, or anthropologists.

Next they are to study any messages that are associated with the extraordinary reports, to ascertain whether they conform with Church teaching.

The third question raised by the document appraises the pastoral implications of the phenomena by studying the fruits of the reported apparitions. Miraculous physical healings, conversions, vocations, and a return to the sacraments are considered to be good fruits.

In September of 1888 at Castelpetroso, Italy, Fabiana Cecchino and Serafina Giovanna Valentino, both in their thirties, had a vision of the Virgin Mary as Our Lady of Sorrows. After some time, news of the occurrence reached Msgr. Macarone-Palmieri, bishop of the Diocese of Bojano, where Castelpetroso is located. He was called to Rome for the business of his diocese, and while he was there, he updated the Holy Father on what was going on at Castelpetroso, adding that he would have liked the apparitions to have been confirmed by some clear sign. The pope asked if he did not think the apparitions in themselves were signs and requested that the bishop return to Castelpetroso and provide a new report. The bishop did as he had been directed and went back to Castelpetroso, and with the archpriest of Bojano, he saw the Virgin three times.

Not all approvals are so easy. For the most recent episcopal approval of an apparition, and the only one in the history of the United States, Bishop David L. Ricken of Green Bay, Wisconsin, initiated an investigation in 2009 in which a team of three renowned Mariologists examined the merits of the 1859 claims of Adele Brise, a Belgian farmworker who reported that she saw the Virgin Mary on three occasions and began to spread Our Lady's messages of conversion and catechesis. The team of investigators pored over thousands of pages of historical documents and accounts of miraculous cures and deep conversions. Some of the miracle accounts related to the Great Peshtigo Fire of 1871 and how the shrine was miraculously spared. In what was the most devastating fire in the history of the United States, much of the eastern side of Wisconsin became engulfed in flames. In the small town of Robinsonville (now Champion), locals gathered at the shrine of Our Lady of Good Help to pray and participate in a procession and prayers to the Virgin Mary that they might be spared as the fire raged around them. In miraculous fashion, the shrine and its property were the only land not torched for as far as the eye could see; even the white picket fence surrounding the small plot of land had been charred. After the commission concluded, Ricken decided that there was enough evidence to declare with confidence that this supernatural event was "worthy of belief" and contained nothing contrary to the teachings of the Church. He made the historic announcement of approval on December 8, 2010, at the Shrine of Our Lady of Good Help:

> I declare with moral certainty and in accord with the
> norms of the Church that the events, apparitions and

locutions given to Adele Brise in October of 1859 do exhibit the substance of supernatural character, and I do hereby approve these apparitions as worthy of belief (although not obligatory) by the Christian faithful.[33]

Unlike most modern apparition investigations, Ricken did not have the benefit of being able to interview the visionary or talk to firsthand witnesses. In the case of the famed apparition claims at Medjugorje, the Vatican investigative commission, beginning on March 26, 2010, had a different set of challenges. The local bishop already had given a negative judgment and repeatedly made known his displeasure with the events in question, and the national conference of bishops had intervened on top of that, issuing its 1991 Zadar Declaration:

On the bas[is] of studies made so far, it cannot be affirmed *Non constat de supernaturalitate* [not established as supernatural] that these matters concern supernatural apparitions or revelations.

The investigative commission, headed by Cardinal Camillo Ruini, vicar general emeritus for the Diocese of Rome, and composed of fifteen members of various disciplines, had to review the thousands of messages attributed to the Virgin and collected over thirty years and to interview all the seers. In the meantime, the Catholic world (with its thirty million pilgrimages made to the small town in Bosnia-Herzegovina) awaited an answer with bated breath. In stark contrast, the investigation into the Wisconsin apparitions was carried out under the radar with even some locals unaware of the reported prodigious events at the shrine a century and a half earlier.

At the time of the Medjugorje investigation, the apparition reports were still occurring. This would typically preclude the

CDF from issuing an outright positive judgment out of pastoral concern that if the Church publicly favored the supernaturality of the events and they later turned out to be a hoax, the Church's authority in these matters would be ridiculed, compromised, and disregarded in general and specifically on future judgments of miraculous claims. In a few select cases in history, such as the Church-approved apparitions in Betania (Venezuela), Kibeho (Rwanda), and Itapiranga (Brazil), the local bishop issued positive statements while the events were still going on, bracketing the years in question, saying that the events during a specific period were worthy of belief.

There are three traditional categories of apparition judgments that relate most importantly to the supernatural character of the event: "not worthy of belief," "approved," and "nothing contrary to the faith" (see figure 1 on page 59). The negative judgment category that asserts that the event is not worthy of belief is given by the Latin formulation *constat de non supernaturalitate*, that is, "It is established that there is nothing supernatural." The negative criteria delineated in *Normae Congregationis* are:

1. Glaring errors in facts
2. Doctrinal errors attributed to God or Mary
3. Pursuit of financial gain
4. Gravely immoral acts committed by the visionary
5. Psychological disorders or tendencies in the visionary

Although Catholics are never obliged to believe in an apparition, even if it is declared to be authentic, they are required to submit themselves to the prudential judgment of the competent ecclesial authority when an apparition is declared false.

The positive judgment, which confirms that the event is worthy of belief, is given by the Latin formulation *constat de supernatu-*

ralitate, that is, "It is established that there is something supernatural." The positive criteria delineated in *Normae Congregationis* are:

1. Moral certainty/great probability of the miracle
2. Positive evaluation of the qualities of the visionary
3. Positive evaluation of the content of the revelations
4. Healthy devotion and spiritual fruits

According to the International Marian Research Institute,[34] there are four criteria that determine whether a Marian apparition is to be approved:

1. There must be moral certainty, or at least great probability, that something miraculous has occurred. The commission may interview the visionaries, call other witnesses, and visit the site of the events.
2. The subjects who claim to have had the apparition must be mentally sound, honest, sincere, of upright conduct, obedient to ecclesiastical authorities, and able to return to the normal practices of the Faith (such as participation in communal worship and reception of the sacraments).
3. The content of the revelation or message must be theologically acceptable, morally sound, and free of error.
4. The apparition must result in positive spiritual assets that endure (prayer, conversion, and increase in virtue).

For an apparition to be declared authentic, it is not enough for the messages to be free from doctrinal error. There have been many cases of claimed apparitions involving messages that are sound and are not contrary to the Faith, but other factors, such as the pursuit of financial gain, lack of obedience, or psychological conditions, are present that rule out the possibility of a supernatural cause.

When an apparition is approved, the Blessed Virgin Mary can be venerated in a special way at the site, although neither this veneration nor even the acknowledgment of the supernatural event is required of Catholics.

The third apparition category is the one of uncertainty, calling for a "wait and see" stance. This judgment is given in the form of the Latin phrase *non constat de supernaturalitate*, that is, "It is *not* established that there is something supernatural." The vast majority of investigated apparitions receive this assessment when the investigative committee cannot at that time make a definitive conclusion. An apparition with such a designation might or might not be of supernatural origin. While there is no proof of the phenomenon originating from anything but natural causes, none of the negative criteria are fulfilled and the supernatural cause is not ruled out.

The local bishop will assess pastorally the best path forward and sometimes will give encouragement to the cult that has arisen around the alleged phenomenon (not to be confused with approval of the supernatural character). The associated messages may be approved for publication, and pilgrimages may be allowed at this stage. In some cases, the local ordinary might deem it appropriate to consider the events worthy of faith expression. If the matter is still being investigated, the bishop could permit public worship while continuing to be vigilant in ensuring that the devotions do not wander in deviant directions. Many *non constat* cases result in the limiting rather than the encouraging of the devotion.

In what continues to be one of the most popular unapproved apparition claims of all time, the events at San Sebastián de Garabandal (commonly referred to simply as Garabandal), Spain, from 1961 to 1965 have left some faithful awaiting in hope the upgrade of the ecclesial judgment of the Church. During those years four young schoolgirls claimed to have received visions and messages from St. Michael the Archangel and the Virgin Mary. There were thousands of claimed visions of Mary with some activity witnessed by thousands and captured in photographs and on live film.

Four successive bishops of Santander have viewed the supernatural character of Garabandal as having no proof of being authentic. In 1993, José Vilaplana, Bishop of Santander, provided a judgment of *non constat* — that is, not established as being supernatural in origin. Regarding these alleged events, he stated, "All the bishops of the diocese from 1961 through 1970 asserted that the supernatural character of the said apparitions, that took place around that time, could not be confirmed [*no constaba*]."

In an official note of July 8, 1965, Bishop Eugenio Beitia of Santander wrote:

We point out, however, that we have not found anything deserving of ecclesiastical censorship or condemnation either in the doctrine or in the spiritual recommendations that have been publicized as having been addressed to the faithful, for these contain an exhortation to prayer and sacrifice, to Eucharistic devotion, to veneration of Our Lady in traditional praiseworthy ways, and to holy fear of God offended by our sins. They simply repeat the common doctrine of the Church in these matters.

The bishop of Santander, who had asked for a more explicit declaration from the Holy See on the matter, reaffirmed that he and his predecessors had never approved or encouraged the devotion or even given its promoters their blessing in a sign of approval. On March 10, 1996, the Sacred Congregation wrote in reply and insisted that the decision rests in the hands of the competent ecclesial authority, the local bishop.

It should be noted that there have only been three phenomena since the beginning of the twentieth century that received negative judgments from initial episcopal investigations and were later upgraded to a *constat* judgment with the interest of a subsequent bishop in reexamining the case. The controversial 1945 Amsterdam apparitions received by Ida Peerdeman experienced a reversal by Bishop Jozef Marianus Punt of Haarlem of a previous "established as not supernatural" judgment that had been acknowledged in 1974[35] and later republished in 2006[36] by the CDF.

Another miraculous event with a reversal (also coincidentally featuring the Virgin under the title Our Lady of All Nations) was the controversial locution and bleeding statue of Our Lady of Akita, Japan, from 1973 to 1981, which originally received a *non constat* judgment from a first commission of inquiry initiated by Bishop John Shojiro of Niigata. When Bishop Ito consulted with Cardinal Ratzinger, the head of the CDF, Ito expressed such a strong belief in the authenticity of the events that he was encouraged by Ratzinger to form a second commission, after which Ito declared on April 22, 1984:

> After the inquiries conducted up to the present day, one cannot deny the supernatural character of a series of unexplainable events relative to the statue of the Virgin honored at Akita (Diocese of Niigata). Consequently I authorize that all of the diocese entrusted to me venerate the Holy Mother of Akita.

The apparition remains controversial due to the dramatic and negative messages about apocalyptic natural disasters and the future of the Church: "cardinals opposing cardinals, bishops against bishops." It remains debated whether Bishop Ito had given approval most specifically to the bleeding statue–related events of Akita verified by science or to the entirety of the events, including the content of the messages.

When an apparition's authenticity is later called into question, the devotion might not be encouraged or emphasized as much. The visionary of Akita, Sr. Agnes Sasagawa, in old age has chosen to withdraw from the public eye and live in private as this devotion to Our Lady has lessened over time. The president of the Japanese Bishops' Conference, Peter Seiichi Shirayanagi, in an interview with the Catholic magazine *30 Days*, said, "The events of Akita are no longer to be taken seriously. We think they do not now have a great significance for the Church and Japanese society."[37]

In one extremely rare case, that of the nineteen visions of the Virgin Mary to the Carmelite novice Teresita Castillo and the phenomenon of rose petals appearing marked with holy images in Lipa City, Philippines, the bishops' commission in 1951 ruled "established as not supernatural," and later the devotion was banned. In 2005, Most Rev. Ramon C. Arguelles, D.D., archbishop of Lipa, resurrected it with an official kickoff with "increased activity and devotion," and in 2009 he lifted the 1951 ban on the public veneration of Our Lady, Mediatrix of All Grace. Despite the negative judgment (reaffirmed by the Vatican in a final statement in 2010), veneration of Mary under that title was still officially permitted in Lipa. In an unprecedented turn of events, during a June 2015 homily at San Sebastian Cathedral, Archbishop Arguelles stated, "I declare today what I always have at heart: Mary, Mediatrix of All Grace of Lipa is worthy of belief." He then followed up on September 12, 2015, as part of the feast day celebrations in Lipa, with the release of an official statement of approval declaring "that the events and apparition of 1948, also known as the Marian phenomenon in Lipa, and its aftermath even in recent times do exhibit supernatural character and is worthy of belief." He presented the approval as an acknowledgment of the *sensus fidelium* and great Marian devotion of the people of the Philippines, but did not cite any new evidence for the case or mention collaboration with the CDF in reversing the decision of a higher authority.

It is worth noting that while it is possible that a judgment of a miraculous event could in fact be changed from a positive statement of "worthy of belief" to a negative statement from one bishop to the next with the uncovering of new information over time, this has never happened in the history of the Church and the odds of its occurrence are in practice almost zero. Such a decision would confuse the faithful and weaken the perception of the authority of the Church in such matters.

A bishop's decision regarding private revelation usually does not attempt to give an interpretation of the events or the associated messages. All such investigations aim to determine whether public devotion should continue to be held in those places.

In a statement in *The Activities of the Holy See* (1996), it was noted that the Congregation for the Doctrine of the Faith was studying apparition-related phenomena and that "alleged apparitions are frequently joined with claims of supernatural messages, and with weeping statues of the Blessed Virgin Mary or of saints." The statement reiterated the responsibility of local bishops to conduct investigations and produce judgments, and it restated the CDF's role as one of "guidance and vigilance."[38]

Figure 1 on the following page summarizes the investigative process for the approval of miracles.

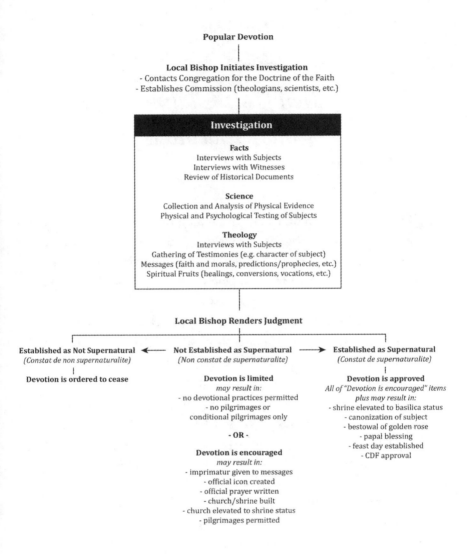

Popular Devotion

Local Bishop Initiates Investigation
- Contacts Congregation for the Doctrine of the Faith
- Establishes Commission (theologians, scientists, etc.)

Investigation

Facts
Interviews with Subjects
Interviews with Witnesses
Review of Historical Documents

Science
Collection and Analysis of Physical Evidence
Physical and Psychological Testing of Subjects

Theology
Interviews with Subjects
Gathering of Testimonies (e.g. character of subject)
Messages (faith and morals, predictions/prophecies, etc.)
Spiritual Fruits (healings, conversions, vocations, etc.)

Local Bishop Renders Judgment

Established as Not Supernatural
(Constat de non supernaturalite)

Devotion is ordered to cease

Not Established as Supernatural
(Non constat de supernaturalite)

Devotion is limited
may result in:
- no devotional practices permitted
- no pilgrimages or
conditional pilgrimages only

- OR -

Devotion is encouraged
may result in:
- imprimatur given to messages
- official icon created
- official prayer written
- church/shrine built
- church elevated to shrine status
- pilgrimages permitted

Established as Supernatural
(Constat de supernaturalite)

Devotion is approved
All of "Devotion is encouraged" items
plus may result in:
- shrine elevated to basilica status
- canonization of subject
- bestowal of golden rose
- papal blessing
- feast day established
- CDF approval

Figure 1.
Investigative Process for Approval of Miracles

CHAPTER 4

Trends in Claims
of the Miraculous

Since the Council of Trent, after which miraculous claims first
began to be thoroughly investigated, the number of claims
has been fairly consistent throughout the centuries. Marian apparitions are perhaps the most documented and studied of all
miracle types, and analysis of the data can provide an overview
of the trends. According to Internet site MiracleHunter.com, 132
claims were made in the sixteenth century, followed by 127 in
the seventeenth century, 40 in the eighteenth century, and 129
in the nineteenth century. In the twentieth century, there was a
veritable explosion of activity as 750 visions of the Virgin Mary
were claimed[39] (see figure 2 on page 61).

To put these numbers into perspective, consider how very
few apparitions in the twentieth century enjoy any sort of approval. (For an apparition to be considered fully approved, the
local bishop must affirm the supernatural character of the event.)
The Vatican, subsequent to the investigation and approval of the
local ordinary, has given some form of recognition to four apparitions: Our Lady of the Rosary (Fátima, Portugal, 1917), the Virgin
with the Golden Heart (Beauraing, Belgium, 1932), the Virgin
of the Poor (Banneux, Belgium, 1933), and Mother of the Word
(Kibeho, Rwanda, 1981). Seven additional apparitions have been
investigated and approved by the local ordinary without having

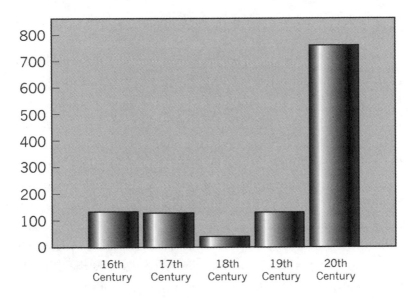

Figure 2.
Apparition Claims since the Council of Trent (1545–1563)

yet received a formal sign of Vatican recognition: Our Lady of All Nations (Amsterdam, Holland, 1945); Our Lady, Mediatrix of All Grace (Lipa, Philippines, 1948); Our Lady of Akita (Akita, Japan, 1973); Our Lady, Reconciler of Peoples and Nations (Betania, Venezuela, 1976); Our Lady of Cuapa (Cuapa, Nicaragua, 1980); Our Lady of the Rosary (San Nicolás, Argentina, 1983); and Our Lady, Queen of the Rosary (Itapiranga, Brazil, 1994). The Coptic Church, which follows an approval process very different from that of the Roman Catholic Church, relying exclusively on prayerful discernment, has recognized four apparition events, all without messages given at the site. Another twenty or so apparitions enjoy an initial permission for faith expression from the local bishop, but their supernaturality has never been verified. All in all, only about 4 percent of all reported apparitions in the twentieth century have received even the lowest level of approval of faith expression by the local ordinary.

Throughout history, many apparitions around the world have been celebrated on the local level in the construction of shrines and regional feasts and commemorations. Fr. Paolo Scarafoni, rector of the European University of Rome and professor of theology at Rome's Pontifical Regina Apostolorum University, recognizing the millions of faithful affected by these claims, although acknowledging the lack of official approval, notes that "the door should not be closed on those but [they] should be studied slowly before final judgment is made." Fr. René Laurentin, foremost Mariologist and author of the *Dictionary of the Apparitions of the Virgin Mary*, says that fifteen apparitions had been officially recognized by the Church, but Fr. Salvatore Perrella, assistant dean of faculty at the Pontifical Theological Faculty Marianum and an expert in Marian apparitions, says only nine have been recognized.[40] MiracleHunter.com identifies at least twenty-eight apparitions throughout history that were positively judged by a local bishop's commission, sixteen of which have received some form of Vatican recognition.[41]

The United States and Canada have experienced many alleged apparitions throughout history, starting with a legend involving first U.S. president George Washington,[42] but only the 1859 apparitions to Adele Brise in Robinsonville, Wisconsin, have ever been approved as worthy of belief by ecclesiastical authorities. Of the more than one hundred claims of apparitions in the twentieth century, only the apparitions of Our Lady of America in Ohio in the 1950s have received even an approval of faith expression.

Between 1900 and 1980, there were 401 Marian apparition claims throughout the world. During this period, there were only 27 reports (6 percent) from the United States and Canada (see figure 4 on page 65).

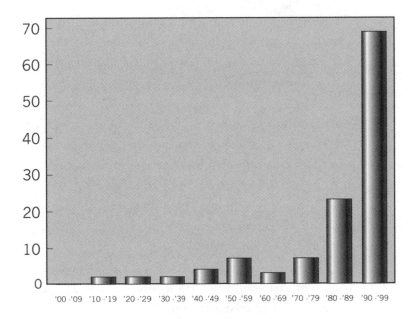

Figure 3.
Apparition Claims by Decade in the United States
and Canada, 1900–2000

Several alleged apparition events from this span of years are particularly noteworthy:

- Cora Evans was a Mormon who became a Catholic in 1935 and experienced visions of Jesus, the Virgin Mary, and saints. She developed a devotion to the Mystical Humanity of Christ, and her beatification cause has been opened.[43]

- Claude Newman was imprisoned for shooting and killing a citizen of Mississippi, where he lived. While incarcerated, he saw a Miraculous Medal worn by another prisoner and asked to wear it. He allegedly received a vision of the Virgin Mary, who counseled him to seek a Catholic priest. After doing so, he learned the Catholic Faith, converted, and influenced several other prisoners before his execution in 1944.[44]

- Mary Ann Van Hoof began her claims of seeing the Virgin Mary in Necedah, Wisconsin, in 1949. Her visions, which became apocalyptic in tone and contained predictions of a UFO arrival, were condemned in 1955. A shrine was completed in 1975 and is currently staffed by an Old Catholic offshoot sect.[45]

- In 1970, Veronica Leuken created a stir in Bayside, New York, with her claims of visions of Our Lady and saints. Her ecstasies lent credence to the belief that a supernatural event was indeed occurring. The messages she relayed made controversial assertions, including the allegation of the presence of an imposter pope in Rome, and they resulted in her receiving a negative judgment in 1986. A shrine still exists in New York that commemorates these occurrences.[46]

After 1980, the frequency of claims of apparitions throughout the world not only tripled from the previous eight decades (from an average of more than five per year to more than fifteen per year), but the reports in the United States and Canada have dramatically increased (from less than one per year to almost five per year; see figure 3 on page 63). The reports from the rest of the world have not increased in such explosive fashion, as the North American events have made up a much larger percentage of the total number of claims worldwide (from 6 percent to 29 percent; see figure 4 on page 65).

The choice of 1980 as the dividing point is not arbitrary. The number of apparition claims in the 1980s alone in the United States and Canada (twenty-three) were nearly equal to the previous eight decades combined (twenty-seven). No previous decade had more than six claims. Something different was happening in the 1980s.

1900–1979   **1980–2000**

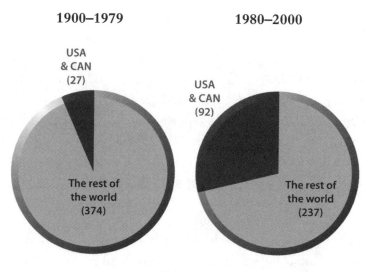

Figure 4.
Total Worldwide Claims of Apparitions in the Twentieth Century

With the proliferation of apparition reports at the end of the twentieth century, the Church reacted with concern about the effects of the focus on such phenomena. The U.S. bishops addressed this issue in a 1996 Special Assembly for America of the Synod of Bishops (*Encounter with the Living Jesus Christ: Way to Conversion, Communion, and Solidarity in America*):

Within the church community, the multiplication of supposed "apparitions" or "visions" is sowing confusion and reveals a certain lack of a solid basis to the faith and Christian life among her members. On the other hand, these negative aspects in their own way reveal a certain thirst for spiritual things, which, if properly channeled, can be the point of departure for a conversion to faith in Christ.[47]

EXPLANATION OF TRENDS

The increase in apparition claims at the end of the twentieth century and the particular growth in the United States could be reflective of many factors. One basic explanation of the dramatic change in the frequency of reports centers on the question of whether the world truly needed the intercession of the Mother of God in a special way at that time. Is it simply the case that the Virgin Mary has been appearing more often? It might not be possible to assess the state of the modern world as compared with other eras in history and its resulting need for divine intervention, but the legitimacy of the claims can be examined. To discern the reality of these apparition claims, the only objective criteria on which to rely are the investigations and prudential judgments of the Church.

All ninety-two alleged apparition claims of the last two decades of the twentieth century in the United States and Canada were declared either "not supernatural" or "not established as supernatural" (most without any approval of the messages or of faith expression) or went uninvestigated, which implies such a lack of solid basis for supernaturality in the first place that they did not even merit the Church's attention. In five of the North American cases declared "not established as supernatural," a local ordinary released a statement with some "wait and see" remarks or allowed the publication of the messages as not contrary to faith and morals. These cases were Mariamante (United States, 1987, Apostolate of Holy Motherhood), Carol Nole and Barbara Matthias (Santa Maria, California, 1988), Joseph Januszkiewicz (Marlboro, New Jersey, 1989), Nancy Fowler (Conyers, Georgia, 1990), and Dory Tan (Marmora, Ontario, Canada, 1990).

It must be acknowledged that the Church is extremely slow in rendering positive judgments and will typically not give approbation to an ongoing apparition. For example, in the case of the 1664 apparitions to Benedicta Rencurel, a shepherdess in France, the Holy See did not release an official approval until 2008. Such a traditionally slow discernment process could certainly keep several of the not-approved or not-condemned apparitions from the 1980s and 1990s under consideration for some time. Improvement in awareness through more media coverage with the advent of modern communication technologies has enabled more reports of visions, messages, signs, and healings to be widely discussed by the increasingly miraculous-minded Catholic faithful. In the 1980s alone, hundreds of books and periodicals were published, video documentaries and audiotapes were produced, and results of investigations were disseminated. This greater exposure might represent a heightened interest in these happenings but does not explain such a dramatic increase in alleged phenomena themselves, other than to suggest that it inspired some charlatans, the mentally unstable, attention seekers, or other pious frauds to be swept up in the fanaticism.

Another theory for the spike in activity relates to the end of the millennium. Fear of the end times inspired many apocalyptic claims, predictions, and new concerns. With uncertainty abounding and many fearing calamity or expecting the return of Christ, prophecy was prevalent. Author Mark Garvey, in his book *Searching for Mary: An Exploration of Marian Apparitions across the U.S.*, assessed this phenomenon:

I think [the alleged apparitions'] popularity in the 90s had a lot to do with the approaching end of the millennium. People in general, and particularly those who believed in signs and portents, saw the coming year 2000 as a significant watershed moment, a moment ripe for something historically, and religiously, significant to happen.[48]

The data seems to back this view of the increase in claimed messages of the Virgin Mary. In the first decade of the twenty-first century, there were only thirty-seven known claims made worldwide, about a quarter of the number from the previous decade.

One very possible explanation for the explosion of miraculous claims could be found in the confusion about the changes in the Church's restriction on the publication of messages associated with alleged apparitions. The Code of Canon Law of 1917 (1399, no. 5) had forbidden publication of anything about alleged supernatural events without the local bishop's approbation. The removal of canons 1399 and 2318 from the Code of Canon Law of 1917 was approved by Paul VI on October 14, 1966, by *Acta Apostolicae Sedis* (AAS) 58 and promulgated on November 15 of that year. As mentioned earlier, this decision, paired with the abolition of the Index of Forbidden Books on June 14, 1966, may have opened the floodgates for people to perceive a newfound license to publish anything without restriction regarding alleged phenomena. With the typical lag time in the dissemination of Church decisions to the faithful, the explosion in the reports of such phenomena beginning in the 1980s could well be attributed to the fact that such phenomena could now apparently be freely written about. What appears to be a dramatic increase in claims could be in reality just more reports coming to light simply because more material was published than ever before.

The fact that the new Code of Canon Law (1983) also addressed this issue and reaffirmed the requirement that bishops approve apparition-related writings seems to corroborate the aforementioned explanation. Canon 823 §1 states:

> In order to preserve the integrity of the truths of faith and morals, the pastors of the Church have the duty and right to be watchful so that no harm is done to the faith or morals of the Christian faithful through writings or the use of instruments of social communication. They also have the duty and right to demand that writings to be published by the Christian faithful that touch upon faith or morals be submitted to their judgment and have the duty and right to condemn writings which harm correct faith or good morals.

With the Index abolished, this canon's restriction on the free circulation of unapproved writings apparently had little effect, because the dramatic rise in apparition reports had already been in full swing for more than a decade by the time the Church addressed this growing concern. In a document released specifically to censure Vassula Ryden, an alleged seer living in Switzerland, the CDF included language and a general instruction that reasserted the moral obligation not to circulate or read writings regarding alleged phenomena:

> II. Regarding the circulation of texts of alleged private revelations, the Congregation states:
>
> 1. The interpretation given by some individuals to a Decision approved by Paul VI on 14 October 1966 and promulgated on 15 November of that year, in

virtue of which writings and messages resulting
from alleged revelations could be freely circulated in
the Church, is absolutely groundless. This decision
actually referred to the "Abolition of the Index of
Forbidden Books," and determined that — after the
relevant censures were lifted — the moral obligation
still remained of not circulating or reading those
writings which endanger faith and morals.

2. It should be recalled however that with regard to
the circulation of texts of alleged private revelations,
canon 823 §1 of the current Code remains in force:
"the Pastors of the Church have the … right to de-
mand that writings to be published by the Christian
faithful which touch upon faith or morals be submitted to their judgment."

3. Alleged supernatural revelations and writings concerning them are submitted in first instance to the
judgment of the diocesan Bishop, and, in particular
cases, to the judgment of the Episcopal Conference and the Congregation for the Doctrine of the
Faith.[49]

The timing of this statement coincides with the peak of apparition activity in the early 1980s across the world and in the
United States specifically.

Perhaps the most compelling evidence for the cause of the
data trend comes in assessing the coinciding of the famed 1981
Medjugorje apparitions and the beginning of the marked spike in
worldwide miracle claims of that period. Beginning on June 24,
1981, Our Lady of Medjugorje (also called "Queen of Peace" and

"Gospa," which is Croatian for "Lady") allegedly began appearing to six Herzegovinian Croat children in Medjugorje, Bosnia, and Herzegovina. Since then Medjugorje has become one of the most popular sites for Catholic pilgrimages. Many of the alleged visionaries of the United States and Canada during the end of the last century, including many of the most widely followed seers, had visited Medjugorje on a pilgrimage before claiming their own visions.

Such popular seers with Medjugorje ties included these:

- Joseph Januszkiewicz (Marlboro, New Jersey, 1989) — A quiet man dedicated to his family, Joseph had a serious accident in 1987 that left him in a wheelchair. Although he was skeptical about the events taking place in Medjugorje, he made a pilgrimage there in 1988 and received a physical healing. His first apparition occurred on March 17, 1989, while he was praying in his backyard. The last message for the people was given on December 4, 1994.[50]

- Fr. Jack Spaulding and his prayer group (Scottsdale, Arizona, 1988) — The apparitions at St. Maria Goretti Parish, in Scottsdale, Arizona, a suburb of Phoenix, began in the late summer of 1988. Nine young people (Gianna Talone Sullivan, Mary Cook, Susan Evans, Steve and Wendy Nelson, James Pauley, Jim Kupanoff, Annie Ross Fitch, and Stefanie Staab) who had been to Medjugorje on pilgrimage approached their pastor, Fr. Spaulding, separately and told him they were hearing voices.[51]

- Estela Ruiz (Phoenix, Arizona, 1988) — After a pilgrimage to Medjugorje, Estela, a wife and mother of seven, claimed to have received apparitions and messages since

December 3, 1988. Mary allegedly appeared as Our Lady of the Americas and gave messages that were read to the crowds of people who went to Estela's home. Estela claimed that Our Lady appeared almost daily in 1989, and all of her seven grown children were converted.[52]

- Theresa Lopez (Denver, Colorado, 1990) — Theresa escaped from a life of drugs, alcohol, and financial problems after her transformation following a pilgrimage to Medjugorje when she claimed her first locutions of the Blessed Virgin Mary. She began traveling around the country as a promoter of the Medjugorje phenomenon. Among her public apparitions was one event attended by six thousand pilgrims who had come to see the Blessed Virgin at Lookout Mountain.[53]

- Nancy Fowler (Conyers, Georgia, 1990) — From October 13, 1990, to October 13, 1998, many thousands of people went to see the "Visionary of Conyers" as she reported that Jesus sent his Mother to communicate heavenly messages calling all of humanity, but especially those in the United States, to conversion. She traveled around the country and abroad, bearing witness to these revelations. Many of her alleged mystical experiences were written down. Her visions began after a pilgrimage to Medjugorje.[54]

- Joseph Reinholz (Hillside, Illinois, 1990) — A retired railroad worker and widower, Joseph suffered from blurred vision and occasional blindness. He visited Medjugorje, and when he returned home, his sight gradually returned to normal. After a second pilgrimage, as foretold by one of the seers, Joseph found a crucifix at Queen of Heaven cemetery and prayed at the site for two years. On August 15, 1990, the Blessed Virgin Mary allegedly began appearing to him there.[55]

• John Leary (Rochester, New York, 1993) — A retired Kodak chemist and devout Catholic, Leary claimed to have received more than thirteen volumes of messages from Jesus and Mary since his 1993 trip to Medjugorje.[56]

• Gianna Talone Sullivan (Emmitsburg, Maryland, 1994) — One of the original nine seers in Fr. Jack Spaulding's Thursday Night Prayer Group based in Scottsdale, Arizona, Gianna claimed to have received messages from the Blessed Mother. Allegedly Our Lady first spoke to her on June 4, 1988, in Medjugorje and eventually began to appear to her beginning on December 19, 1989, during the Thursday prayer meetings in Scottsdale's St. Maria Goretti Church. Gianna and her husband relocated from Scottsdale to Emmitsburg in November 1993 at the reported request of the Blessed Mother.[57]

• Maureen Sweeney-Kyle (Cleveland, Ohio, 1996) — A housewife and grandmother, Maureen claimed that, following her pilgrimage to Medjugorje, Jesus and the Blessed Mother had been appearing to her almost daily since 1985. The Holy Love movement and shrine were established based on her alleged apparitions.[58]

• Kathryn Ann Clarke (Illinois and Ireland, 2004) — In September 2001, on pilgrimage in Medjugorje, Kathryn, a fiction writer and mother of six, "spoke with

Jesus conversationally" when receiving Communion.[59] She later reported visions of Jesus and the Virgin Mary and, under the pseudonym "Anne, a Lay Apostle," has recorded her locutions in a series of volumes titled *Direction for Our Times*, which has received an imprimatur from Bishop Leo O'Reilly of the Diocese of Kilmore.

This data does not, of course, suggest that on this basis the apparitions at Medjugorje should be considered false or looked upon with suspicion. Many investigated and approved apparitions have been the objects of aping locally or nationally. In Belgium, for example, following the two back-to-back approved apparitions at Beauraing and Banneux in 1932 and 1933, respectively, there was a marked spike in claims in the following year as thirteen of the fifteen worldwide supposed visions of the Virgin Mary occurred in Belgium.[60] Lourdes is perhaps more famous for impostor children coming forward who wanted to emulate St. Bernadette Soubirous. Fr. Leonard Cros, S.J., an early chronicler of the apparitions, identified more than thirty cases of local mimicry.[61] Similar increases in claims surrounded the apparitions at Knock, Ireland, and Fátima, Portugal. In Kibeho, Rwanda, the visionaries who saw the "Mother of the Word" were all from the same school and inspired other schoolchildren there to make similar claims.

Although, in the past, examples of mimicry might have been limited to those areas surrounding the region of an apparition, in modern times the same psychological phenomenon of emulation might be in play for those who frequent apparition sites on pilgrimage, even from a great distance. Medjugorje has uniquely enjoyed an unprecedented flood of international interest and special attention from the faithful in the United States. Since the events began in 1981, more than thirty million pilgrims, including many

Americans, have made their way to the now developed small village in Bosnia-Herzegovina. The fame of the alleged apparitions can be attributed in part to their consistent, long-running, widely translated, and well-distributed messages that have been examined in several investigations, including that of the 1991 Zadar Conference of Yugoslavian Bishops. The decision declared the apparitions *non constat de supernaturitalitate* (not established as supernatural) rather than condemning them outright with a *constat de non supernaturalitate* (established as not supernatural) judgment, thereby insinuating that the messages contained nothing contrary to faith and morals.

Pilgrimages were likewise approved if they were conducted privately and did not operate on the assumption that Our Lady was certainly appearing. With a booming economy in the United States, curious pilgrims went in droves to see what they could see or to attain a miracle. Likewise modern communication technology made the dissemination of messages easier. The United States has been a specially targeted place of outreach for the Medjugorje message, as Caritas, a spiritual center in Birmingham, Alabama, has been established around the frequent and consistent visits of one of the seers, Marija Lunetti (Pavlović).[62] Another of the visionaries, Ivan Dragicevic, has sought to spread the Medjugorje message specifically to the United States by visiting parishes from October through February. The services he facilitates typically consist of his testimony, prayer, and an onsite apparition.[63] (Note: On October 21, 2013, the apostolic nuncio in the United States, Cardinal Vigano, wrote to USCCB General Secretary Msgr. Jenkins, calling for the restriction of these presentations and any other events that take the credibility of the alleged apparitions for granted.[64]) Additionally, Mir Centers, dedicated to spreading the messages of Our Lady at Medjugorje, popped up throughout the United States in the 1980s and 1990s.

Even considering the important role of miracles in the history of the Church, the data spike in alleged miraculous phenomena at the end of the last century provides a good backdrop for reemphasizing the importance of both following the prudential judgment of competent ecclesiastical authorities and understanding the proper role of the miraculous. Although apparitions may bolster the faithful, provide special insights, and aid at crucial moments in history, they must always point the faithful toward Christ.

CHAPTER 5

Healing Miracles and the Canonization Process

O f the various types of miraculous phenomena experienced throughout the world today, the most common are medical healings. Throughout the Gospels, Jesus performs an incredible number of healing miracles: giving sight to the blind (Mt 20:29–34; Mk 10:46–52), enabling the mute to speak (Lk 11:14), curing leprosy (Mt 8:1–4; Mk 1:40–42), and raising people from the dead (Mt 9:18, 23–25; Mk 5:35–42). He helped friends — curing Peter's mother-in-law (Mt 8:15) and raising Lazarus from the dead (Jn 11:44) — and even would-be enemies: according to the Gospel of John, in the chaos surrounding his arrest, Jesus cared to heal the ear of the Jewish high priest's servant Malchus after Peter had severed it. Throughout the Gospels, the Lord cured every kind of ailment and disease (Mt 9:35). According to the Gospel of Matthew, Jesus' concern and care for the sick fulfilled the prophecy of Isaiah: "He took our infirmities and bore our diseases" (Mt 8:17; cf. Is 53:4).

Since the very beginnings of Christianity, the Church has sought to bring Christ's concern for the sick into its ministry. Jesus sent out the apostles in pairs to the towns in Galilee to heal the sick and to cast out demons (Mk 6:7–13). In the many accounts of cures found in the Acts of the Apostles, Peter and Paul used healing miracles (5:12) to validate their message and convert souls. From the infant Church to the modern day, the world has witnessed the healing effect of faith put into action.

Skeptics have questioned whether psychosomatic effects and autosuggestion play any role in healing the body as claimed in miracle cures. In her book *Nothing Short of a Miracle*, Patricia Treece recounts several university studies that consider the effects of faith on healing. Duke University, Fordham University, Agnes Scott College, the Institute for Psychobiological Research (London), and UCLA have all conducted studies to measure the positive effect of faith on healing. These studies have shown that prayer can have numerous positive effects on the human body, including on blood cell count, skin temperature, blood pressure, and brain waves.[65] Prayer has been tested both when others pray for the subject and when the subject prays for himself. One 2002 study reported in the *Annals of Behavioral Medicine* linked the length of time AIDS patients survived to the amount they prayed.[66] Cases of the miraculous cures of infants, such as the return to life of a stillborn child in the Ven. Fulton Sheen beatification cause, demonstrate the power of prayer for others.

Saints have gained renown throughout the ages as intercessory agents with the power to bring about miracles both in life and death. Codices such as *Liber Jacobi*, which catalogues the great miracles of St. James granted throughout Europe, were kept to collect the favors, healing miracles and otherwise, bestowed on the faithful through the aid of particular saints. As in the case of his famed Camino, the great Spanish pilgrimage route on the way to the basilica and tomb of St. James in Santiago de Compostela, Spain, many people travel to the burial spots and shrines of the great saints to petition for their blessings and intercession.

Many shrines dedicated to the Virgin Mary under her apparition titles have become powerful locations for people seeking miraculous cures. Each year millions of pilgrims visit the shrine of Our Lady of Guadalupe for help in view of her miraculous image at the place commemorating her 1531 apparitions to St. Juan Diego. And, as mentioned earlier, although the site has not been officially confirmed by the Church as an authentic place of Marian apparitions, more than thirty million pilgrims have gone to the small town of Medjugorje in Bosnia-Herzegovina since 1981. There are many noteworthy stories, some verified by medical doctors, of dramatic healings of people who have approached God in faith through the the intercession of the Virgin.

The most renowned location for medical healings is, of course, the shrine of Our Lady of Lourdes in France that was built to commemorate the eighteen apparitions of the Virgin, under the title the Immaculate Conception, received by fourteen-year-old Bernadette Soubirous in 1858. During an apparition on February 25, the Virgin described the location of a healing spring and instructed Bernadette to dig in the mud, revealing the underground water source. Since that time millions of pilgrims have gone to Lourdes and followed the instruction of Our Lady of Lourdes to "drink at the spring and wash in it." There have been thousands of medically inexplicable cures recorded, but very few have been validated.

Unlike any other apparition site, Lourdes hosts its own medical commission, called the International Lourdes Medical Committee (abbreviated in French to CMIL), where miracle claims can be submitted and verified. Only the smallest fraction has passed the commission's rigorous tests. To minimize biases in its judgments, the panel of medical doctors is composed of international physicians who serve for short periods. The process for verification is extremely stringent, allowing only the most authentic and indisputable miracles to pass the standards of approval. The cures must be proven to be instantaneous, complete, and lasting and not the product of medical intervention.

In 2013, the Sanctuary of Lourdes announced the sixty-ninth official miracle, the curing of an Italian woman, Danila Castelli (b. 1946), following her visit to the shrine in 1989. At age thirty-four, Danila started having spontaneous and severe hypertensive crises. She also suffered a number of other serious health problems and underwent a hysterectomy, an annexectomy, and a partial pancreatectomy. Changing her initial plan to go to Mayo Clinic, she and her husband went to Lourdes in May 1989. After experiencing an extraordinary feeling of well-being in the baths, she reported to the Lourdes Office of Medical Observations her alleged instantaneous cure and began the rigorous process of miracle verification. After five meetings over the years, the bureau certified the cure with a unanimous vote, saying that she had been cured in a complete and lasting way of the syndrome she had suffered and not from treatments and the surgeries she received. The Lourdes International Medical Committee certified that the cure "remains unexplained according to current scientific knowledge." On June 20, 2013, Msgr. Giovanni Giudici, bishop of Pavia, the diocese where Danila Castelli lives, declared the "prodigious-miraculous" character of this cure.[67]

Miracles also go through such an intense and rigorous process when they are being offered as proof of the intercessory power of a potential saint in a canonization cause. The vast majority (99.9 percent) of all miracles used in modern canonization causes are medical healings.

The only modern example of a nonmedical miracle used in a cause for canonization is one of food multiplication. Children from a nearby orphanage came to the Ribera del Fresno parish hall each evening to be fed, and poor families in the parish would come to the door to receive a meal. On January 25, 1949, there was not enough food for all the orphans and the poor, with less than a pound and a half each of meat and of rice available.

The cook knelt and prayed for the intercession of then-Blessed John Macias, who had cared for the poor while he was alive, and after she started cooking the rice, she noticed that the pot was overflowing and needed two more pots to hold the extra. For four hours the pot provided rice until all who came, almost two hundred persons, were fed. Twenty-two people witnessed the miracle.[68]

When potential saints are being vetted before ascending to the canons of holy men and women, the Church not only thoroughly examines their lives for heroic virtue but also requires proof of their intercessory power to ensure that they are in heaven. St. John Paul II (1920–2005) is appreciatively or disparagingly called the Great Saintmaker, not only for having in fact canonized more saints than any pope in history at the time of his pontificate (1,338 beatifications and 482 canonizations) but also for having relaxed the rules for canonization. Instead of needing three miraculous intercessions, potential saints are required to have only two attributed to them. Additionally, St. John Paul II retired the role of devil's advocate (*advocatus dioaboli*), the person assigned to arguing the case against a sainthood cause. He wanted to increase the speed of the canonization process — not water it down — because we need examples of holiness now more than ever. John Paul II himself went through the very process of canonization he helped develop, when a Costa Rican woman with one month to live was healed of a brain aneurysm through his intercession on May 1, 2011, as she watched his beatification ceremony on television.

In the Catholic Church, the act of canonization is reserved to the Holy See and occurs at the conclusion of a long process requiring extensive proof that the person proposed for canonization lived and died in such an exemplary and holy way that he or she is worthy to be recognized as a saint. The Church's official recognition of sanctity implies that these persons are now in heavenly glory and that they may be publicly invoked and mentioned officially in the liturgy of the Church, most especially in the Litany of the Saints.

Canonization involves a decree that allows veneration of the saint in the liturgy of the Roman Rite throughout the world. For permission to venerate on a local level, only beatification is needed, not canonization.[69]

Currently there are more than three thousand worldwide open causes that have passed the initial investigations of local bishops.[70]

THE HISTORY OF CANONIZATION

Throughout history, the Church has canonized more than ten thousand saints, a group comprising martyrs who gave up their lives affirming their faith in Christ and confessors who demonstrated heroic virtue during their lifetimes. The Canon of the Mass contains the names only of martyrs and of the Virgin Mary and St. Joseph (since 1962).

By the fourth century, however, confessors began to be venerated publicly. Their names could be found in the lists of liturgically venerated saints, and their tombs were given special distinction, similar to the treatment of the martyrs' places of rest. If their cultus (popular devotion) received approval by the local bishop in a "local canonization," they could be venerated publicly.[71]

Unless a martyr was definitively known by the faithful to have truly died for the Faith, veneration of someone who had the reputation of martyrdom still required authorization. To reduce the error in recognizing nonauthentic martyrs, St. Cyprian (d. 258) insisted that great care and diligence go into the inquiries of the claims surrounding martyrs' deaths, including their lives of faith and their motivations. Testimonies from trials and witness accounts were all used in the verification process.[72]

St. Augustine of Hippo (d. 430) indicated that the bishop of the diocese in the location of the act of martyrdom would be responsible for establishing a canonical process to investigate the claim thoroughly. The resulting findings of the inquiry would be reviewed by the metropolitan, who, after detailed examination of the cause, and conferring with the suffragan bishops, would issue a statement on whether the candidate was worthy to be recognized as a martyr worthy of public veneration.[73]

Before any outward signs of recognition could take place, including the building of an altar over the saint's tomb, translating the saint's relics to a church, promoting a prayer, or celebrating a local feast day, there must be a formal inquiry into the holiness of the person and any miracles claimed to have occurred through his or her intercession.

The formal recognition of a saint would be applicable only for the relevant local diocese or ecclesiastical province but could extend elsewhere as the saint's cultus grew.

CANONIZATIONS IN THE MIDDLE AGES

In the early centuries of the Church, the bestowing of sainthood on an individual was something left to local dioceses and regions. If a saint was celebrated beyond the area where he or she was from, it would be because of the spread of the saint's legend or reputation for sanctity. To make such recognition more official and known to the universal Church, the Holy See began to make authoritative decisions regarding canonizations. Sainthood causes were decided with greater frequency by the judgment of the popes. William Smith, author of *A Dictionary of Christian Antiquity*, notes that the canonization of St. Ulric, bishop of Augsburg, by Pope John XV in 993 is the first unchallenged example of a papal canonization of a non-Roman saint.[74] Walter of Pontoise, who was canonized by Hugh de Boves, the archbishop of Rouen, in 1153 was the last known saint in Western Europe to have been canonized by an authority other than the pope.[75]

A decree of Pope Alexander III, in 1170, gave the prerogative to the pope thenceforth, so far as the Western Church was concerned.[76] Three years later, after denouncing a case of the veneration of an unworthy would-be saint, Pope Alexander decreed: "You shall not therefore presume to honor him in the future; for, even if miracles were worked through him, it is not lawful for you to venerate him as a saint without the authority of the Catholic Church."[77] His text, establishing the pope as the authority in canonization declarations, was confirmed by the papal bull of Innocent III in 1200, issued on the occasion of the canonization of St. Cunegunde.

CANONIZATIONS BETWEEN THE EIGHTEENTH AND TWENTIETH CENTURIES

As mentioned earlier, Prospero Lambertini elaborated on the procedural norms issued by Pope Urban VII (1623–1644)[78] in *De Servorum Dei Beatificatione et de Beatorum Canonizatione* in 1740. The document asserted that the events in question must present themselves to human reason as being truly extraordinary and beyond the scope of natural causes. Miracles validated for use in canonization causes must involve a serious illness at a stage where it is not liable to disappear on its own or due to medical treatment. The cure must be instantaneous, complete, and lasting.

Lambertini's five-volume work set the standards for canonization from his time until the twentieth century. Its substance was incorporated into the Code of Canon Law of 1917.[79]

The Roman Curia's Sacred Congregation of Rites was established on January 22, 1588, by Pope Sixtus V and its functions reassigned by Pope Paul VI on May 8, 1969. The congregation was charged with the supervision of the liturgy and other sacraments and with the process of canonization of saints. With the reforms of Paul VI, it was divided into the Congregation for the Causes of Saints and the Congregation for Divine Worship.[80]

SINCE 1983

Pope John Paul II's apostolic constitution *Divinus Perfectionis Magister* of January 25, 1983, and the norms issued by the Congregation for the Causes of Saints on February 7, 1983, for its implementation on the diocesan level continued the work of simplification already initiated by Pope Paul VI. After these changes took place and throughout the pontificate of John Paul II, the number of canonizations substantially increased.

One of the major changes involved the removal of the office of the promoter of the Faith (*promotor fidei*), popularly known as the devil's advocate (*advocatus diabolic*), who was required to present a case against canonization. He would take a skeptical view of the candidate's character, look for holes in the evidence, and argue that any miracles attributed to the candidate were fraudulent. The devil's advocate opposed God's advocate (*advocatus Dei*, also known as the promoter of the cause), whose task was to make the argument in favor of canonization. While the office has officially been retired, in select cases testimony might be requested against a sainthood cause. Aroup Chatterjee, the author of the book *Mother*

Teresa: The Final Verdict, testified against the late nun as a devil's advocate. The British-American columnist Christopher Hitchens was famously asked to testify against her beatification in 2002, a role he would later describe as being akin to "representing the Devil, as it were, pro bono."[81]

The task of the devil's advocate is now performed by the promoter of justice (*promotor iustitiae*), who is in charge of examining the accuracy of the inquiry on the saintliness of the candidate.

The new norms also reduced the number of required miracles. While speeding up the process dramatically overall, the reduction also saves money on medical experts and streamlines the efforts of the promoters of the cause and of those in the Vatican who verify the miracles. Canonization causes are expensive due to the required manpower to read and manage the reports of miraculous cures and other elements of the process. Some potential saints cannot be presented due to the lack of an official sponsor or funds to process the paperwork.

STEPS TO CANONIZATION

Once a candidate's cause is opened and he or she is termed a Servant of God, the candidate advances to Venerable and then Blessed before finally being declared Saint.

Venerable/Heroic in Virtue

The cause for a saint's canonization is typically initiated by a petitioner and set up in the location where the person died or sometimes in Rome. This petitioner, or *actor*, may be an individual or a group (e.g., a parish, a religious congregation, a diocese, an association of lay faithful, or even a civil body) with the desire and means to finance and promote the cause.

The actor will identify a *postulator* recognized by the competent local bishop where the Servant of God died. A postulator is the lawyer of the cause and representative of the actor before the Congregation for the Causes of Saints (CCS).

It is the task of the actor, through the postulator, to request that the bishop launch a formal diocesan investigation. At the same time, the CCS designates a protocol number to refer to the case. If the bishop of another diocese were to act as the competent bishop for the cause of someone who died outside the jurisdiction of his territory, he would have to obtain the decree for the transfer of the competent forum (*competentia fori*) from the CCS.[82]

Before any miracles attributed to the saint's intercession are identified and verified, the CCS must attest to the person's holiness — that is, the candidate must have demonstrated a life of heroic virtue. Once the necessary amount of historical research has been completed, including interviews with witnesses when applicable, a recommendation is made that the candidate be upgraded to the status of Venerable. This is an important step, as it clears away any roadblocks regarding the worthiness of the candidate to be canonized on the basis of virtue.

John Paul II's *Divinus Perfectionis* requires the competent bishop to consult with the bishops of his region about the cause and publish the petition of the postulator. The faithful are to submit any information they might have on the Servant of God. Once the cause is officially initiated, two theologian-censors are chosen to examine the writings (published and unpublished) of the Servant of God, and they must provide a favorable opinion in order for the cause to proceed. After this, the bishop assigns a promoter of justice, whose task is to draw up a questionnaire for witnesses. The CCS then issues a *nihil obstat*, which certifies that no Vatican records indicate anything that would merit a suspension of the investigation.[83]

After obtaining the *nihil obstat*, the bishop, through a diocesan tribunal, examines witnesses, including eyewitnesses to the life of the Servant of God as well as those who have studied their writings. The questionnaire drawn up by the promoter of justice is used to interview them. Proof that there is no existent formal cult at the location of the person's death is ascertained. When the inquiry is complete, two copies of all the proceedings, called the *transumptum*, are sent to the CCS.[84]

At this point, the CCS validates the records of the investigation and appoints to the cause a *relator*, who supervises the writing and publication of the *positio* by a collaborator, who is often the postulator. The positio provides: (1) the biography of the Servant of God based on the transumptum; and (2) the *summarium*, all the testimonies of the witnesses and documents relative to the candidate's life. Historians, theologians, and prelates appointed by the CCS then vote to determine the final result of the cause.

A unanimous decision on the position leads to a formal decree from the CCS on the heroic virtues or martyrdom of the Servant of God, and the decree is typically read before the pope in a public audience. From that moment forward, the Servant of God can be referred to as Venerable.[85]

A candidate who is Venerable does not receive a feast day and cannot have churches built in his or her honor. At this stage, the Church has not definitively declared that the person is undoubtedly in heaven. Devotional materials, such as prayer cards, are permitted to inform and encourage the faithful to pray for the candidate's canonization — namely, through the rendering of a miracle showing the person's intercessory power and thus proving that the person is indeed in heaven.

Blessed

The next step is the declaration of beatification, when the candidate is to be called Blessed. This process can be initiated by a petitioner five years after the death of the would-be saint. The pope himself may waive the required five-year waiting period, as in the case of Mother Teresa of Calcutta and John Paul II. Whereas the Venerable status makes no official assurance that the person is in heaven, beatification establishes that it is "worthy of belief" that the person is with God.

A distinction is made in the process if the Venerable is a martyr or a confessor. For a martyr (*in odium fidei, uti fertur* — presumably killed out of hatred for the Faith), the pope must make an authoritative affirmation of martyrdom, certifying that the Venerable gave up his or her life voluntarily as a witness for the Faith. Cases in which the martyr has acted in a demonstration of heroic charity for the sake of others may be accepted as well.

In the case of confessors who bear witness to their Faith through their lives of heroic virtue (*in fama sanctitatis* — with a reputation for holiness), miracles are required to prove their intercession — that is, as a sign of their presence with and closeness to God, they have acted on behalf of those who besought them in prayer. Oftentimes the canonization cause will collect documentation for many miracles and then select the most certifiable examples to be reviewed and verified in Rome. For the causes of some saints, such as Detroit's Solanus Casey and Montreal's André Bessette, their promoters flooded the approval process with numerous claims to be considered.[86] Often it is hoped that a collective set of miracles will go a long way to establish the person's reputation for holiness.

Almost all miracles used in modern beatification causes are medical. These are the easiest to define certifiably as supernatural interventions and most easily meet the requirements of the Church. To pass muster, the cure must be spontaneous, instantaneous, complete, and lasting. In December 2013, the medical commission of the Congregation for the Causes of Saints (the *consulta medica*) called a healing attributed to Pope Paul VI "unexplainable." Doctors had warned a pregnant California woman of likely brain damage in her unborn child and advised her to abort. The child was later born without any defects, but only when the child reached puberty could doctors be certain of whether the child had made a full recovery without any problem.[87] It is often required that someone who has experienced a miraculous healing pass away (from another cause or condition) in order to guarantee that the disease has not returned. Cancer survivors must pass the five-year mark before they are even considered to have been cured miraculously. In one case, a woman was seemingly cured of cancer through the intercession of Bl. Francis Xavier Seelos, but she died of pneumonia before the required cancer-free years had passed, so her miracle was excluded.[88]

In approved cases, doctors cannot find any natural explanation for the cure (e.g., another illness has somehow affected the first one) and rule out the effect of any related medical interventions.

Cures must meet seven criteria to be considered miraculous:[89]

1. The disease must be serious and impossible (or at least very difficult) to cure by human means.

2. The disease must not be in a stage at which it is liable to disappear shortly by itself.

3. Either no medical treatment must have been given, or it must be certain that the treatment given has no reference to the cure.

4. The cure must be spontaneous.

5. The cure must be complete.

6. The cure must be permanent.

7. The cure must not be produced by any crisis of a sort that would make it possible that the cure was wholly or partially natural.

Most medical doctors involved in these specific cases will not testify to the miracle because it implies that nothing they did helped the patient. It is for this reason that the doctors on the Vatican panel have no connection to the cases on which they render judgments. In 2008, the medical commission for the Congregation for the Causes of Saints, to judge its extraordinariness, featured sixty-two doctors in various specialties. On the local level as well, the investigation is spearheaded by an uninvolved doctor appointed by the bishop.[90]

After a miracle is identified and verified as being without known natural cause, it is then looked at by theologians who try to assess whether the miracle is due to supernatural factors, specifically the intercession of the saint in question. After that, the cause and its miracle claim are evaluated at a special commission of cardinals and bishops, who review the findings of the doctors and theologians. If everything checks out, it is passed to the desk of the pope, who signs off on the case in an official act of authentication. Not until science, faith, and the authority of the Church are behind it will a miracle be considered a proof to be used in a saint's canonization.

Prior to John Paul II's pontificate, two to four miracles were required for beatification and the same number for canonization. In streamlining the process, the Church has brought to light more holy role models for the world to see.

One of the most challenging aspects of identifying a worthy miracle is first establishing that it was worked *exclusively* through the intercession of the would-be saint. It is not uncommon for a person who needs help to ask many friends for a hand, so it seems reasonable that someone facing a life-and-death situation would call on the entire litany of saints if not his or her personal and most effective favorites. Even if the miracle were to be approved as worthy of belief as being beyond natural causes, not being able to pinpoint which saint interceded in the miracle would make it ineligible for use to establish someone's cause for sainthood.

On March 6, 2014, the beatification cause of the Emmy Award–winning media bishop, Ven. Fulton Sheen, took a major step forward when a panel of Vatican experts could not determine a natural cause for the revival of a stillborn baby who had no detectable pulse at birth and for a lengthy period thereafter. The baby's family had prayed exclusively to Sheen and invited others to do the same. The baby survived without defect and matured into a healthy boy.[91]

Under Pope John Paul II, a candidate's beatification normally took place in Rome, where the pope himself would officiate at the ceremony, although he celebrated many of these rites in the country where the candidate for beatification lived, labored, or died. For example, for the 1990 beatification of St. Juan Diego, the visionary of the apparitions of Our Lady of Guadalupe, John Paul II traveled to Mexico City for a Mass attended by millions of faithful. Under Pope Benedict XVI and Pope Francis, a cardinal appointed by the pope has presided over the rite. After the solemn act, the Venerable is referred to as Blessed, but veneration is typically limited to that region or religious community.[92]

Once beatification occurs, the Venerable is now called Blessed or, in Latin, *Beatus* or *Beata*. When a feast day is established, it is observed only in the Blessed's home diocese and the churches or houses of his or her religious order, if the Blessed belonged to one. Parishes may not normally be named in honor of a Blessed, but modern exceptions have been made for Mother Teresa and John Paul II.

Saint

To be taken to the next step, to sainthood, an additional distinct miracle (it cannot be a cure of another ailment in the same person claiming the first) must be identified to show the saint's intercession after his or her death.

The causes of many blesseds from an earlier age remain frozen without the requisite second miracle worked for the modern faithful, who may have forgotten to pray to them. In some rare cases, people are elevated to the altars of the saints through papal prerogative (bypassing the requirement of intercessory miracles), as was St. Peter Faber (1506–1546) in 2013. Some saints from long ago do receive that long-awaited miracle, as in the case of the 2012 canonization of St. Kateri Tekakwitha (d. 1680), when an eleven-year-old boy from Seattle, also a Native American, received through her intercession a miraculous cure from a flesh-eating virus.

There are many *thaumaturgic* ("wonderworking") saints who were renowned for the many miracles they worked during their lives, but none of these can be used for canonization, as they do not establish that the person is in heaven enjoying the Beatific Vision. As a result of being officially declared *sanctus*, the saint receives a feast day, which may be celebrated anywhere within the Catholic Church (although it may or may not appear on the General Calendar or local calendars); parish churches and official shrines may be built to honor the saint; and the faithful may freely and without reservation celebrate and venerate him or her.

Although recognition of sainthood by the pope does not directly concern a fact of divine revelation, the faithful are to recognize a canonization as an infallible declaration with its guarantee by the magisterial teaching authority of the Church.

EQUIVALENT CANONIZATION

On several occasions, popes have opted not to follow the ordinary judicial process of canonization if the cultus (popular devotion) was such that the person was already being venerated locally. This action by a pope is known as equivalent (or equipotent) canonization or "confirmation of cultus."The Blessed's liturgical cult is extended to the universal Church. According to Prospero Lambertini, there are three conditions for such an equivalent canonization: an ancient cultus, a general constant attestation by trustworthy historians to the virtues or martyrdom of the person, and continuous recognition as a worker of miracles.

Like numerous popes before him, Pope Francis has added saints through equivalent canonizations. He named Angela of Foligno and Peter Faber saints in 2013, and on April 3, 2014, he signed decrees recognizing: St. José de Anchieta, a Spanish-born Jesuit who traveled to Brazil in 1553 and became known as the Apostle of Brazil; St. Marie de l'Incarnation, a French Ursuline who traveled to Quebec in 1639 and is known as the Mother of the Canadian Church; and St. François de Laval, who arrived in Quebec twenty years after St. Marie de l'Incarnation and became the first bishop of Quebec. Later that year he elevated to sainthood "the Good Pope," John XXIII, without the traditional second miracle required. Instead, Francis based this decision on John XXIII's merits for the Second Vatican Council.[93] On Divine Mercy Sunday, April 27, 2014, John XXIII and John Paul II were declared saints. During his first visit to the United States, Pope Francis canonized famed California missionary priest Junipero Serra on September 23, 2015, at the Basilica of the National Shrine of the Immaculate Conception, Washington, DC, waiving the requirement of a second miraculous intercession.

Cardinal Angelo Amato, the prefect of the Congregation for the Causes of Saints, said in a December 2013 interview, "Equivalent canonization, though not frequent, is not rare in the Church." The best-known persons declared saints through equivalent canonization are Gregory VII, Gertrude of Helfta, Peter Damian, Cyril and Methodius, John Damascene, the Venerable Bede, Albert the Great, Thomas More, and John of Avila.[94]

CHAPTER 6

Biblical Miracles

In *Miracles: A Catholic View*, Dr. Ralph McInerny suggests that it is through creation itself that God reveals himself to us, because in the design of the things of this world we are able to discern the work of his divinity. Beyond our knowing God through creation, he has revealed himself to people — starting with Adam and Eve and the Old Testament prophets.

The great miracle at the beginning of the New Testament, the Virgin Birth (cf. Mt 1:18–25), is the clear fulfillment of God's promise of a sign in Isaiah 7:14 to indicate the birth of the Messiah: "Therefore the Lord himself will give you a sign. Behold, a virgin shall conceive and bear a son, and shall call his name Immanuel." The Incarnation brings revelation to reality in the person of Christ:

> The Christian economy, therefore, since it is the new and definitive covenant, will never pass away; and no public revelation is to be expected before the glorious manifestation of Our Lord Jesus Christ.[95]

With the Incarnation, God unequivocally displays his glory and his love for us (Jn 1:14; 3:16). St. John Paul II taught that salvation is rooted in this greatest of all miracles:

> This reality-mystery embraces and surpasses all the miraculous happenings connected with Christ's messianic

mission. It may be said that the Incarnation is the "miracle of miracles," the radical and permanent "miracle" of the new order of creation. God's entrance into the dimension of creation is effected in the reality of the Incarnation in a unique way. To the eyes of faith it becomes a sign incomparably superior to all the other miraculous signs of the divine presence and action in the world.[96]

The apostles and their official successors bring the mission and words of Jesus Christ in Sacred Scripture to the world. This faithful interpretation and protection of Scripture through the workings of the Holy Spirit constitutes the proper conjunction of Sacred Scripture and Sacred Tradition.

Sacred Tradition and Sacred Scripture make up a single sacred deposit of the Word of God, which is entrusted to the Church. By adhering to it the entire holy people, united to its pastors, remain always faithful to the teachings of the apostles. (No. 10)[97]

To understand properly the role of miracles throughout Scripture and all of Christian history, it is necessary to know the connection of Scripture, Tradition, and the Magisterium (the teaching authority of the Church) and their mutual reliance on each other.

If it is believed that the Holy Spirit is indeed the author of Sacred Scripture, that Scripture is divinely inspired, it is necessary that it is handed on to the Church so that it might be taught without error for our salvation. In the words of St. Paul: "All scripture is inspired by God and profitable for teaching, for reproof, for correction, and for training in righteousness, that the man of God may be complete, equipped for every good work" (2 Tim 3:16–17).

The Old Testament and New Testament are not to be considered separate, competing works but working in unison to announce the divine mission:

God, the inspirer and author of the books of both Testaments, in his wisdom has so brought it about that the New should be hidden in the Old and the Old should be made manifest in the New.[98]

OLD TESTAMENT MIRACLES

The purpose of miracles in the Old Testament is to prepare the way for the coming of Christ the Redeemer and his kingdom.[99] Miracles are seals of the truth of the divine mission to which the sacred writers appealed as proofs that they were messengers of God. Miracles assure us of the presence of God. For the prophet who works them, miracles are clear proof that he comes with the authority of God; they are his credentials as God's messenger.

It is important not to get derailed by the literary form of the Old Testament and considerations of time, place, and culture and assess the writings as mythical literature. There are incredible and meaningful stories — profoundly true and beautifully symbolic — that make up Sacred Scripture. From the seminal moment of God's speaking to Abraham from the burning bush to the prodigious parting of the Red Sea, through which the Israelites crossed to freedom, and from God's providing manna in the desert to the crashing down of Jericho's walls at the sound of trumpets, the wonders of old have shaped history, literature, and faith forever. The miracles of the Old Testament should not be dismissed as impossible or irrelevant. They prepare the path for the arrival of Christ as Redeemer.

In speaking with Moses, God showed him how to demonstrate his authority by divine mandate through the use of miracles:

> Moses answered, "But behold, they will not believe me
> or listen to my voice, for they will say, 'The LORD did not
> appear to you.'" The LORD said to him, "What is that in
> your hand?" He said, "A rod." And he said, "Cast it on the
> ground." So he cast it on the ground, and it became a ser-
> pent; and Moses fled from it. But the LORD said to Moses,
> "Put out your hand, and take it by the tail" — so he put
> out his hand and caught it, and it became a rod in his
> hand — "that they may believe that the LORD, the God of
> their fathers, the God of Abraham, the God of Isaac, and
> the God of Jacob, has appeared to you." (Ex 4:1–5)

And God gave his promise to enable Moses to work miracles
through him so that his power would be made manifest:

> Then he said, "Behold, I make a covenant. Before all your
> people I will do marvels, such as have not been wrought
> in all the earth or in any nation; and all the people among
> whom you are shall see the work of the LORD; for it is a
> terrible thing that I will do with you." (Ex 34:10)

Moses demonstrated the power of God to the Pharaoh in the
summoning of the ten plagues against Egypt:

Water turning to blood — Exodus 7:14–25
Frogs — Exodus 8:2–14
Gnats — Exodus 8:16–18
Flies — Exodus 8:21–32
Death of livestock — Exodus 9:2–7

Boils — Exodus 9:8–12
Hail with fire and thunder — Exodus 9:14–33
Locusts — Exodus 10:12–19
Darkness — Exodus 10:21–20
Death of all firstborn — Exodus 11:1–8; 12:29–30

In the Israelites' Exodus out of Egypt, they witnessed other signs and wonders, including the parting of the Red Sea (Ex 14:21–31), the flowing of water from the rock at Rephidim (Ex 17:5–7), and the Manna in the desert (Ex 16:14–35), a foreshadowing of the bread given to us by Christ in the Eucharist.

Descriptions of miracles performed by prophets occur frequently in the Hebrew Bible, some similar to the wonders described in the New Testament. There are accounts of people raised from the dead, such as when Elijah raised a widow's dead son (1 Kings 17:17–24) and when Elisha restored to life the son of the woman of Shunem (2 Kings 4:18–37).

There are food miracles, as when the prophet Elijah was fed by ravens (1 Kings 17:4–6), when Elisha multiplied the poor widow's jar of oil (2 Kings 4:1–7), and when a hundred men were fed with twenty barley loaves and some ears of corn at Gilgal (2 Kings 4:42–44).

Many healing miracles are recounted as well in the Hebrew Scriptures, as when Jeroboam's hand instantly withered and then was restored (1 Kings 13:4–6), when Naaman was instantly healed of leprosy (2 Kings 5:10–14), and when the Syrian army was healed of blindness at Samaria (2 Kings 6:18–20).

Other stories speak of miraculous protection from danger, including Shadrach, Meshach, and Abednego's deliverance from the fiery furnace in Babylon (Dan 3:10–27), Daniel's protection from hungry lions (Dan 6:16–23), and Jonah's survival in the whale's belly and his safe landing (Jon 2:1–10).

Like the prophets of the Old Testament, but superseding them in word, deed, and mission, Jesus used signs and wonders in the New Testament to establish His authority.

NEW TESTAMENT MIRACLES

Following the Ascension, the apostles worked many miracles in Christ's name. The conversion of St. Paul (Gal 1:11–16), due to his "visions and revelations" from the Lord (2 Cor 12:1–6), is perhaps the miracle with the single greatest impact on the spread of Christianity. Paul of Tarsus, formerly known as Saul, a "zealous" Pharisee who "intensely persecuted" the followers of Jesus, after a flash of light, the sound of a voice, and temporary blindness (Acts 9:3–9), became the greatest missionary and evangelist for the Christian Faith, spreading the gospel far and wide while founding several churches in Asia Minor and Europe. Additionally, letters he wrote to various Christian communities became fourteen of the twenty-seven books in the New Testament. In the Acts of the Apostles, Paul is reported to have worked great miracles, including raising the young Eutychus from the dead (Acts 20:9–12).

Peter is also depicted as working great signs and wonders and converting thousands with his testimony (Acts 4:4), and the deacon Stephen is mentioned as being filled with "grace and power" in working miracles (Acts 6:8).

As the working of miracles was essential for the establishment of the Church and for validating it with the show of a divine mandate, Our Lord appealed to miracles as a conclusive proof of His divine mission (John 5:20, 36; 10:25, 38). His many "mighty works and wonders and signs" (Acts 2:22) manifest that the kingdom is present in Him and attest that He is the promised Messiah (CCC 547).

St. Augustine spoke of the miracles of Christ as an aid to help us overcome our human limitations in understanding Christ: "The miracles worked by our Lord Jesus Christ are divine works which raise the human mind above visible things to understand what is divine."[100] Being outside the common experience of nature and beyond the power of humanity, they convey the reality of the presence and power of God. According to Pope Paul VI's *Dignitatis Humanae* (Declaration on Religious Freedom), Jesus "supported and confirmed his preaching by miracles to arouse the faith of his hearers and give them assurance" (no. 11).

The Purpose of Jesus' Miracles

Christ's miracles are not intended to satisfy people's curiosity or desire for magic (CCC 548). Rather, the miracles of the New Testament serve as proofs of Christ's divinity. From the Council of Ephesus in 431, St. Cyril writes to Nestorius in his third letter that Christ performed wonders to demonstrate his divinity.[101] In the Council of Constantinople in 553, Christ's two natures, of God and of man, are seen in his performing of miracles and in his Passion, as it was necessary to affirm that the miracle-working Word of God and the man Jesus, who was born of a woman and voluntarily suffered death, were one and the same.[102]

There are three main types of miracles performed by Jesus in the Gospels:

1. Those in the spiritual realm, such as casting out demons
2. Those that affected people, including healings
3. Those that controlled nature, such as walking on water

Spiritual

According to the three Synoptic Gospels (Matthew, Mark, and Luke), Jesus performed many exorcisms of those possessed by demons, including casting out seven demons from Mary Magdalene (Mk 16:9; Lk 8:2). In the exorcism at the synagogue in Capernaum, Jesus removed an evil spirit who identified him: "What have you to do with us, Jesus of Nazareth? Have you come to destroy us? I know who you are, the Holy One of God!" (Mk 1:21–28; Lk 4:31–37).

In a following instance, in which the possessed did not identify Christ by name, the Pharisees accused Jesus of being a demon himself. Faced with a blind and mute man possessed by evil spirits, Jesus both cast out the demon and healed the man so that he could talk and see. People who knew Jesus from his hometown asked in bewilderment, "Could this be the Son of David?" The Pharisees said that Jesus' power to drive out demons emanated from Beelzebul, ignoring that Jesus had also healed the man of his blindness and muteness. Jesus caught them in their nonsensical accusation: "A house divided against itself cannot stand" (cf. Mt 12:22–32; Mk 3:20–30; Lk 11:14–23).

In the exorcism of the Gerasene demoniac, witnesses began to see and understand the great power that Jesus commanded. When he met the demoniac who had been wildly roaming the hills, Jesus asked the man's name and was told in response, "Legion … for we are many." The devils asked to be expelled into a herd of swine, which Jesus permitted, and the swine rushed down the bank into the lake and were drowned. The swineherds reported in the town what had transpired, and when the townsfolk saw that the man was now sane, they pleaded with Jesus to leave, "for they were seized with great fear" (Mt 8:26–37; Mk 5:1–17; Lk 8:26–37).

In another story of spiritual cleansing, Jesus acted from afar. In Matthew 15:21–28 and Mark 7:24–30, a Canaanite woman approached Jesus to ask him to heal her daughter, but Jesus said, "I was sent only to the lost sheep of the house of Israel." When the woman replied, "Lord, yet even the dogs eat the crumbs that fall from their masters' table," Jesus told her that her daughter was healed, and when the woman returned home, she found that indeed it was so.

Jesus used these miraculous interventions against evil to inspire the faith of the crowds. A boy possessed by a demon was brought forward to Jesus immediately after Jesus' Transfiguration. The boy was said to have completely lost control of his actions and emotions and would fall into water and fire. Jesus' disciples were unsuccessful in casting out this demon. When the boy's father questioned Jesus' ability to work the miracle, he condemned the people as unbelieving, saying, "All things are possible to him who believes." When the father believed, Jesus healed his son (Mt 17:14–20; Mk 9:14–29; Lk 9:37–43).

Physical

The largest group of miracles mentioned in the New Testament involves the cures Jesus performs in "all the cities and villages, teaching in their synagogues and preaching the gospel of the kingdom, and healing every disease and every infirmity" (Mt 9:35). There are many descriptions of varying levels of detail of Christ's healing leprosy, restoring sight to the blind, and enabling paralytics to walk again. In one of the most famous accounts, Jesus cures a woman suffering from hemorrhaging (Mt 9:20–22; Mk 5:24–34; Lk 8:43–48). The Gospels report that on the way to the house of Jairus, a ruler of the synagogue, Jesus was approached by a woman who had been suffering from bleeding for twelve years.

104 EXPLORING THE MIRACULOUS

When she touched his cloak, she was instantly healed. Jesus felt the power leaving him and turned about to identify her. When the woman admitted reaching out to him for a cure, he said, "Daughter, your faith has made you well; go in peace" (Lk 8:48). When Jesus later passes through Gennesaret, all those who touch his garment are healed (Mt 14:34–36; Mk 6:53–56).

Healing the lepers

In one story of healing a leper, after curing the man, Jesus instructs him to offer the requisite ritual sacrifices prescribed by the Deuteronomic Code and Priestly Code. Most importantly, it seems, he is to speak to no one on the way; but the formerly leprous man disregarded the command, thus increasing Jesus' fame. Jesus then withdrew to deserted places but was followed there (Mt 8:1–4; Mk 1:40–45).

In an episode in the Gospel of Luke, while on his way to Jerusalem, Jesus meets ten lepers who seek his assistance. He sends them to the priests, and they are healed as they go. Only one of them, a Samaritan, comes back to thank him, and Jesus asks, "Were not ten cleansed? Where are the nine?" (Lk 17:11–19).

Giving sight to the blind

In addition to describing many cases of Jesus' curing leprosy, the Gospels describe four cases of his healing the blind.

Each of the synoptic Gospels tells of Jesus' healing a blind man near Jericho as he passed through that town shortly before his Passion. Matthew (20:29–34) describes a similar account of two blind men being healed outside of Jericho but gives no names. Mark tells only of a man named Bartimaeus being present and healed:

And they came to Jericho; and as he was leaving Jericho with his disciples and a great multitude, Bartimaeus, a

blind beggar, the son of Timaeus, was sitting by the road-
side. And when he heard that it was Jesus of Nazareth, he
began to cry out and say, "Jesus, Son of David, have mercy
on me!" And many rebuked him, telling him to be silent;
but he cried out all the more, "Son of David, have mercy
on me!" And Jesus stopped and said, "Call him." And they
called the blind man, saying to him, "Take heart; rise, he
is calling you." And throwing off his cloak he sprang up
and came to Jesus. And Jesus said to him, "What do you
want me to do for you?" And the blind man said to him,
"Master, let me receive my sight." And Jesus said to him,
"Go your way; your faith has made you well." And immediately he received his sight and followed him on the
way. (Mk 10:46–52)

By this time, the renown of Christ as a healer has grown, as
shown in the Gospel of Matthew (9:27–31), which reports Jesus'
healing two blind men in Galilee who called him "Son of David."
Jesus touched their eyes and restored their sight.

In the Gospel of John, the topic of having a condition such
as blindness from birth is discussed (9:1–12). In response to the
question about whose sin caused the illness, Jesus stated that the
man in the account was born blind not because he or his parents
sinned. Rather than cure the man with one action, as in other
healings, Jesus mixed spittle with dirt to make a muddy paste,
which he placed in the man's eyes. Jesus then asked the man to
wash his eyes in the pool of Siloam, after which he could see.

The account of Jesus' healing the blind man in Bethsaida is
told only in the Gospel of Mark (8:22–26).

Paralytics

In Capernaum, a paralytic on a mat had to be lowered through
a roof to reach Jesus, who told him to get up and walk, and the

man did so. Jesus also boldly told the man that his sins were forgiven, a claim that the Pharisees disputed. "But Jesus, knowing their thoughts, said, 'Why do you think evil in your hearts? For which is easier, to say, "Your sins are forgiven," or to say, "Rise and walk"? But that you may know that the Son of man has authority on earth to forgive sins' — he then said to the paralytic — 'Rise, take up your bed and go home.' And he rose and went home" (Mt 9:2–7).

A similar cure is described in the Gospel of John as the healing the paralytic at the pool of Bethzatha. Jesus likewise instructs the paralytic to take up his mat and walk (Jn 5:1–18).

Raising the dead

Perhaps in a foreshadowing of his own dramatic victory over death, Jesus performs the greatest healing miracle of all — raising the dead. In three instances recorded in the Gospels, Jesus brings someone back from the grave. In one account (Mk 5:21–43), Jairus, a major patron of a synagogue, asks Jesus to heal his daughter, but she dies before he arrives. Jesus tells Jairus that she is only sleeping and wakes her with the words "Talitha cumi" ("Little girl, I say to you, arise").

A young man from Nain, the son of a widow, is brought out for burial. Jesus sees the mother and in pity tells her not to cry. He approaches the coffin and tells the young man inside to rise, and so he does (Lk 7:11–17).

In the most famous of account of Jesus showing his divine power in raising someone from the dead, he restores life to his close friend Lazarus, who had been dead for four days (Jn 11:1–44).

Nature

In addition to the miracles contemplated by St. Thomas Aquinas and St. John Chrysostom, suggesting that Christ manipulated the sun and the moon to create an extended eclipse at his Crucifixion and guided the star of Bethlehem to signal his birth,[103] Jesus' command over nature in less cosmic ways clearly demonstrated that in his divine power, all of nature was subject to him.

Several of Jesus' great miracles pertain to food. As his first public miracle and a clear demonstration of the intercessory power of Mary as the Mother of God, the wedding feast at Cana shows the compassion of Christ for his hosts when they are running low on wine. He commands that six stone jars be filled with water and a sample of the water be drawn out and taken to the master of the banquet, who judges it to be the best wine of the banquet (Jn 2:1–11).

When Peter, James, and John are unsuccessful in catching fish for their dinner and their livelihood, Jesus intervenes by instructing them to cast their net on the other side of the boat. The miraculous draft of fishes takes place early in Jesus' ministry, and as a result of it, Peter, James, and John join Jesus to become fishers of men (Lk 5:1–11).

Perhaps to teach his disciples a lesson, Jesus again demonstrates his power over nature when, in frustration with a fruitless fig tree that cannot provide him with food, Jesus curses the tree, causing it to wither (Mk 11:12–14, 20–21).

Certainly the greatest food-related miracle wrought by Jesus is the feeding of the five thousand. When Jesus is informed of the shortage of food among the many who have gathered to hear him speak, he prays to God the Father, and with only five loaves of bread and two fishes, he is able to feed thousands of men, along with an unspecified number of women and children. It is the only miracle, apart from the Resurrection, depicted in all four Gospels (Mt 14:13–21; Mk 6:31–44; Lk 9:10–17; Jn 6:5–13).

Following the feeding of the five thousand is the story of Jesus' walking on water (Mt 14:22–33; Mk 6:45–52; Jn 6:16–21), in which Peter, fearfully and semi-successfully, leaves the boat to join Jesus in participating in this great miracle. In another boating story in which Jesus shows his dominion over nature, the apostles wake him from his sleep to beg him to save them from a violent storm. He promptly quiets the wind and the waves and pointedly asks, "Do you still have no faith?" (Mt 8:23–27; Mk 4:35–41; Lk 8:22–25).

The Resurrection

Without a doubt, the greatest miracle recorded in Sacred Scripture is the Resurrection of Christ, for on it the entirety of Christian belief and existence rests. It is so important that, without it, all the rest of the miracles before and after would be rendered absolutely meaningless. Paul sums up the contingency of the practice of Christianity on the physical reality of the Resurrection when he declares: "[I]f Christ has not been raised, then our preaching is in vain and your faith is in vain" (1 Cor 15:14). According to Paul, the Resurrection of Christ is not merely a symbol or a suggestion that Christ lives on in our memory and practice of faith. The Resurrection is the definitive and ultimate proof of Christ's divinity and authority (see CCC 651):

> The empty tomb and the linen cloths lying there signify in themselves that by God's power Christ's body had escaped the bonds of death and corruption. (CCC 657)

Leading up to that incredible day, a series of events culminating in his death on the Cross seemed to mark Jesus' ministry as an abject failure. His Passion, from the Agony in the Garden to the Scourging at the Pillar to the Way of the Cross and the Crucifixion, reminds us of the incredible sacrifice for our sins that was not understood fully by Christ's disciples and friends. The Sunday after the Crucifixion, Mary Magdalene, Mary the wife of Cleopas, and Salome go to the tomb, expecting to pay their respects and anoint the body of their slain Master. An angel in white sitting in the empty tomb with the stone rolled away tells them to inform the others that Jesus has risen:

> Now after the sabbath, toward the dawn of the first day of the week, Mary Magdalene and the other Mary went to see the tomb. And behold, there was a great earthquake; for an angel of the Lord descended from heaven and came and rolled back the stone, and sat upon it. His appearance was like lightning, and his clothing white as snow. And for fear of him the guards trembled and became like dead men. But the angel said to the women, "Do not be afraid; for I know that you seek Jesus who was crucified. He is not here; for he has risen, as he said. Come, see the place where he lay. Then go quickly and tell his disciples that he has risen from the dead, and behold, he is going before you to Galilee; there you will see him. Behold, I have told you." So they departed quickly from the tomb with fear and great joy, and ran to tell his disciples. And behold, Jesus met them and said, "Hail!" And they came up and took hold of his feet and worshiped him. (Mt 28:1–9)

In the first of many post-Resurrection visions, Jesus appears to Mary Magdalene, who tells the others about it, but they dismiss her: "But when they heard that he was alive and had been seen by her, they would not believe it" (Mk 16:11). He sees them many times after that, and all their doubts, even those of Thomas, are allayed. When he appears in subsequent visions, his disciples know him in the breaking of the bread in such places as on the way to Emmaus.

In the triumph of the Cross over sin and the victory over death as evidenced by the greatest miracle human history has ever known, Jesus redeemed the sins of the world. His Church was just on the brink of being born at Pentecost, and his apostles were sent out with a mandate to spread the gospel and work miracles for generations to come.

CHAPTER 7

Miracles of the Saints

From the earliest days of Christianity, the followers of Christ set out to work miracles in his name. Christ sent out these apostles — from the Greek *apostello*, "to send forth" or "to make a delegate" — in pairs to towns in Galilee (Mk 6:7–13). They were to heal the sick, drive out demons, and preach the gospel to all nations (Mt 28:19; Mk 13:10). The miracles wrought by the apostles established their authority and validated their message as authentic.[104]

In the Acts of the Apostles following Pentecost, Peter first worked a miracle by healing a crippled beggar:

> But Peter said, "I have no silver and gold, but I give you what I have; in the name of Jesus Christ of Nazareth, walk." And he took him by the right hand and raised him up; and immediately his feet and ankles were made strong. And leaping up he stood and walked and entered the temple with them, walking and leaping and praising God. (Acts 3:6–8)

Then Peter wins the attention of the crowds with a speech that is understood by each person there in his own language (Acts 3:11–26). His convincing words affirmed Christ's Resurrection and reminded the people of his miraculous works, resulting in the conversion of many: "But many of those who heard the word believed; and the number of the men came to about five thousand" (Acts 4:4).

The apostles continued to work wonders. Without much detail, we find out that "many signs and wonders were done among the people by the hands of the apostles" (Acts 5:12) and that Stephen, "full of grace and power, did great wonders and signs among the people" (6:8). Later in the account, Peter heals Aeneas at Lydda (9:32–35) and raises the disciple Tabitha from the dead: "But Peter put them all outside and knelt down and prayed; then turning to the body he said, 'Tabitha, rise.' And she opened her eyes, and when she saw Peter she sat up" (9:40).

Later in the Acts of the Apostles, more miracles abound. Peter is rescued from prison (12:3–19), and Paul is credited with working miracles: "And God did extraordinary miracles by the hands of Paul" (19:11). While Paul was preaching, a young boy named Eutychus fell out a window to his death. Paul embraced him and raised him from the dead, and his family "took the lad away alive, and were not a little comforted" (20:12).

The miracles of the apostles in Sacred Scripture belong to public revelation, but the signs and wonders of the Church — now in the form of private revelation — have continued beyond the Acts of the Apostles through the great works and lives of the saints.

As Paul notes in his first letter to the Corinthians, the Spirit works differently in each of us, and some have incredible mystical gifts bestowed upon them:

To each is given the manifestation of the Spirit for the common good. To one is given through the Spirit the utterance of wisdom, and to another the utterance of knowledge according to the same Spirit, to another faith

by the same Spirit, to another gifts of healing by the one
Spirit, to another the working of miracles, to another
prophecy, to another the ability to distinguish between
spirits, to another various kinds of tongues, to another
the interpretation of tongues. All these are inspired by
one and the same Spirit, who apportions to each one
individually as he wills. (1 Cor 12:7–11)

In beatifications and canonizations, the Church celebrates
verified instances in which the saints bring their miracles to the
lives of the faithful. These signs worked after the saints' deaths are
seen as God's way of giving his blessing to their recognition as
holy men or women, and they assure us that these saints are in
heaven. It is not uncommon for the faithful to build friendships
with the saints who work wonders in their lives. In *Nothing Short
of a Miracle*, author Patricia Treece recounts the story of Ven. Solanus Casey, renowned for having worked many miracles during
his lifetime, who claimed a mystical friendship with St. Thérèse of
Lisieux, who worked a physical healing in his life.[105]

We hear the stories of many saints who possessed mystical
gifts, and through written accounts and traditions, we remember
the incredible miracles they worked and the amazing phenomena they experienced. From the Council of Ephesus (431), St.
Cyril's third letter to Nestorius speaks of miracles performed by
the saints:

Finally this same spirit, working glorious miracles through
the hands of the holy apostles as well, glorified Our Lord
Jesus Christ after he ascended into heaven.[106]

The Council of Trent relates the importance of the miracles
of the saints:

Through God's saints miracles and salutary examples are
put before our eyes that we might imitate the life and
customs of the saints and be stirred up to love God and
foster piety.[107]

Many stories of the saints come down to us as legends or the
product of oral histories written down many years after those
saints died. It wouldn't be correct to label their great miracles and
supernatural abilities as mythical, for all things are possible with
God and those blessed with great faith and grace surely can work
wonders. The accounts of these claimed prodigies are so powerful,
though, that it would be quite normal to view them with at least
a slightly skeptical or discerning eye. While fascinating in themselves, these wondrous occurrences exist not for the sake of curiosity or entertainment but to draw people to Christ and his work
of salvation. Without that focus, miracles become mere marvels.

Hagiographies, the stories of the lives of saints, include fantastic accounts of otherworldly abilities. Some saints have been
reported to give off a holy glow. Others have been said to levitate
off the ground in ecstasy or appear in two places at once (bilocation). Still others have exhibited the gift of tongues as modeled
by the apostles after the descent of the Holy Spirit. Like Peter
and Paul in accounts related in the Acts of the Apostles, some
faith-filled saints have been reported to have pulled off the greatest of miracles, raising someone from the dead. As author Patricia
Treece claims in *The Sanctified Body*, "The human body in sanctity
will inevitably reflect its mystical life by unusual energies."[108]

Going back to the New Testament and starting with the
Transfiguration, there have been great examples of illuminations in the stories of Christianity. According to reports, some
supernatural phenomena, including some cases of Eucharistic
miracles and incorruptible bodies, have featured a mysterious

light. Accounts of brilliant lights accompanying saints abound. St. Bonaventure (1221–1274) reported that St. Francis's body was occasionally illuminated in such a way that it gave "witness to the wonderful light that shone within his soul."[109]

A flame was seen hovering over the head of St. Ignatius of Loyola (1491–1556), the founder of the Society of Jesus, while he celebrated Mass. He was thought to be on fire by onlookers but in fact was in deep contemplation.[110] Legends from the life of Bl. Francis of Posadas (b. 1644) of Cordoba, Spain, suggest that he was often seen surrounded by a great light while celebrating Mass and even emitted light from his mouth on occasion.[111] Skeptics question the anecdotal nature of most luminosity accounts.

One of the truly mystifying phenomena reported in the lives of the saints is the ability to rise off the ground in levitation during great ecstasies. The most famous of all saints known for levitation, Joseph of Cupertino (1603–1663), was a poor student who was reluctantly accepted into the Franciscan Order but exhibited great mystical gifts. According to stories of his life, he would rise into the air to the high altar almost daily for adoration of the Blessed Sacrament. He was witnessed in levitation by Pope Urban VIII but was later brought before the Inquisition to determine the source of his flight. He is regarded as the patron saint of aviation.[112]

According to legend, St. Alphonsus Liguori (1696–1787), Doctor of the Church and founder of the Redemptorists, when preaching at Foggia, was lifted several feet off the ground before the eyes of his congregation.[113] St. Angela Merici (1474–1540), founder of the Ursuline Order, was reported to rise off the ground when in adoration of the Blessed Sacrament.[114] The great mystic and Doctor of the Church St. Teresa of Ávila (1515–1582) was endowed with numerous supernatural gifts, including visions, the stigmata, and incorruptibility after death, and she was said to levitate during Mass on occasion, causing the other sisters to try to pin her down.[115] The original written accounts of Teresa's levitations derive primarily from her autobiography. Also, in addition to his other mystical gifts, St. Francis of Assisi is reported to have levitated. Still, in his classic analysis of miracles, *The Physical Phenomena of Mysticism*, English priest Fr. Herbert Thurston reached the conclusion that "the evidence for levitation in the case of some very eminent saints is far from satisfactory."[116]

Several saints have been said to bilocate, allowing them to be witnessed in two places at once. In 1774, St. Alphonsus Liguori claimed to have gone into a trance while preparing for Mass, after which he said that he had visited the bedside of the dying Pope Clement XIV. Bl. Anne Catherine Emmerich (1774–1824), the German mystic and stigmatic, was bedridden for many years but claimed with the help of her guardian angel to have visited many places, including the Holy Land, where she learned details of the life of Christ.[117] St. Martin de Porres (1579–1639), the patron saint of people of mixed race, was likewise said to have had many supernatural abilities, including the gift of healing and communication with animals. Although he never left the Monastery of the Holy Rosary in Lima, Peru, stories recount his presence in Mexico, China, Japan, and Africa, helping the poor.[118] Documentation is much stronger in the case of the famed modern mystic St. Pio (1887–1968), whose bilocation stories are well known. Despite being a cloistered Capuchin friar, various accounts place him in North and South America and throughout Europe, with some reliable witnesses such as bishops having claimed to have seen him in Rome. Likewise reputable testimony has been given about Padre Pio's bilocation to the Hungarian dungeon where Joszef Cardinal Mindszenty was imprisoned in the fifties.[119] Unverifiable stories abound of his visits to hospitals and even to pilots in flight.[120]

Another gift of the spirit claimed by some saints throughout history and modern Pentecostals and charismatics is that of speaking in tongues, also known as *glossolalia*, which may take several forms. In the form demonstrated by the apostles, the speaker talks in a language understood by all listeners. In another, more modern variant, a supposedly mystical language is used that requires an interpreter. Glossolalia also sometimes refers to xenoglossy, the speaking of a natural language previously unknown to the speaker. Rarely, the term may refer to the ability to speak with animals.

The apostles first demonstrated this supernatural ability at Pentecost after the Holy Spirit descended upon them in "divided tongues like fire":

> And they were all filled with the Holy Spirit and began to speak in other tongues, as the Spirit gave them utterance. Now there were dwelling in Jerusalem Jews, devout men from every nation under heaven. And at this sound the multitude came together, and they were bewildered, because each one heard them speaking in his own language. And they were amazed and wondered, saying, "Are not all these who are speaking Galileans? And how is it that we hear, each of us in his own native language? Parthians and Medes and Elamites and residents of Mesopotamia, Judea and Cappadocia, Pontus and Asia, Phrygia and Pamphylia, Egypt and the parts of Libya belonging to Cyrene, and visitors from Rome, both Jews and proselytes, Cretans and Arabians, we hear them telling in our own tongues the mighty works of God." (Acts 2:4–11)

Some Pentecostals and charismatics will pray in an unintelligible "prayer tongue" that is not any particular language or combination of languages. They claim that it is a "language of the spirit," a "heavenly language," or perhaps the language of angels. This variation of speaking in tongues requires someone with the gift of interpretation of tongues. Skeptics regard this as an utterance of meaningless syllables. In 1972, William J. Samarin, a linguist from the University of Toronto, published a thorough assessment of Pentecostal glossolalia. He found that the resemblance to human language was merely on the surface and so concluded that glossolalia is "only a façade of language" and defined Pentecostal glossolalia as "meaningless but phonologically structured human utterance, believed by the speaker to be a real language but bearing no systematic resemblance to any natural language, living or dead."[121]

Several saints are said to have employed the gift of xenoglossy in their preaching, allowing them to reach larger, more diverse audiences. St. Anthony of Padua (b. 1195) was known to be a powerful preacher partly because it was said that in the great crowds who listened to him, everyone, no matter what his country of origin, could understand him.[122] In his missionary travels to India, Japan, and elsewhere, St. Francis Xavier (1506–1552) successfully baptized forty thousand persons, partly due to his supposed ability to communicate with all listeners, regardless of tongue.[123] Another missionary, St. Francis Solano (b. 1549), was able to preach to the tribes of South America in their native dialects.[124]

The greatest of Christ's healing miracles found in the Gospels are, of course, those in which he raises someone from the dead. There are three such instances in the Gospels: the raising of the son of the widow of Nain (Lk 7:11–17), the raising of Jairus's daughter (Mk 5:21–43; Mt 9:18–19, 23–26; Lk 8:40–42, 49–56), and the raising of Lazarus (John 11:1–44). In the Acts of the Apostles, Peter (9:40) and Paul (19:11) each raise someone from the dead as well. Such incredible miracles, however, are not limited to the age written about in Sacred Scripture, as some (known as cessationists) might suggest. St. Anthony of Padua was said to have had this power, having interceded in restoring dozens of people to life. The legends recorded about St. Patrick, the great bishop and missionary to Ireland, mention thirty-nine people having been raised to life through his prayers.[125] The great miracle-working Polish priest St. Hyacinth (1185–1257) exhibited mystical gifts, such as the power of healing, and is said to have brought fifty people back from the grave.[126] St. Vincent Ferrer (1350–1419), a Spanish Dominican, is credited with the conversion of thousands of non-Christians in Europe, no doubt aided by his renown for having raised twenty-eight people from the dead.[127]

CHAPTER 8

Apparitions

A pparitions are perhaps the most unique and controversial of all miracles. They are supernatural, corporeal appearances of Jesus, the Virgin Mary, or saints to one or more persons. Typically they are accompanied by messages for the faithful, at times just for the witnesses themselves but in most other cases for a larger audience — the local community, the country, or the universal Church. It is in this element of private revelation where the potential controversy lies — Church leaders and faithful must determine how they should respond to the instructions, prophecy, and warnings in the content of the messages.

For all the reluctance to embrace apparitions — and certainly there is no moral obligation for any person, Catholic or otherwise, to do so — it is important to recall that such events are found in Sacred Scripture as well. Many visions and miracles are recorded in the Scriptures, including those of angels in both the Old Testament (Jacob wrestles with the angel — Gen 32:22–32) and the New (angels appear to both the Virgin Mary and St. Joseph).

If we include dreams and visions, then at least 120 apparitions are mentioned in the Old Testament.[128] Joseph, son of Jacob and Rachel, was seventeen years old when he had two prophetic dreams that implied his supremacy over his brothers, who in anger plotted his demise (Gen 37:1–11). In the first dream, Joseph and his brothers gathered bundles of grain, and his brothers' bundles bowed to his. In the second dream, the sun (father), the moon (mother), and eleven stars (brothers) bowed to Joseph.

Shadrach, Meshach, and Abednego were delivered from the fiery furnace in Babylon (Dan 3:10–27) by an angel of the Lord who appeared and went into the furnace to drive out the fiery flames, prompting King Nebuchadnezzar to take them out of the furnace and exclaim, "Blessed be the God of Shadrach, Meshach, and Abednego, who has sent his angel and delivered his servants, who trusted in him" (Dan 3:28).

In the New Testament, visions continue to play a role in revelation. At the Transfiguration (Mt 17:1–9; Mk 9:2–8; Lk 9:28–36), during which Jesus is transformed on the mountaintop and becomes radiant, the prophets Moses and Elijah appear next to him. Jesus is then called "Son" by a voice from the sky, from God the Father, as he was after his baptism.

After the Resurrection, Christ appeared to "Cephas [Peter], then to the Twelve" (1 Cor 15:5) numerous times and other times to other disciples, including on the road from Jerusalem to Emmaus (Lk 24:13–35). In the early Church, the deacon Stephen experienced a vision of the heavens open and Christ at the right hand of God the Father (Acts 7:55–56). The conversion of St. Paul (Gal 1:11–16) after his "visions and revelations" from the Lord (2 Cor. 12:1–6) is the seminal miraculous event that turns him into the greatest missionary in Christian history. The book of Revelation, the final book of the New Testament and the primary source of Christian eschatology, relates the visions of St. John.

Beyond the time of the apostles and throughout Christian history, there have been many stories of spiritual dreams and visions. The great saint and founder of the Salesians, John Bosco (1815–1888), was known for his dreams. At age nine, he had a dream in which his friends got into a schoolyard fight. When he went to break it up by punching the aggressors, he saw the Virgin

Mary, who told him, "Not by blows will you reach them but by kindness"; then the boys turned first into wolves and then into lambs. The dream became very influential in his decision to become a priest and in his work with children, which earned him the title "The Father and Teacher of Youth."

John Bosco's most famous dream some years later became known as the dream of the two pillars. In the dream he saw a group of ships at sea. The main vessel had the Holy Father aboard, and this represented the Church. Rough seas and attacking ships threatened the safety of the Bark of Peter, but two great pillars appeared out of the waves, one with the Eucharist and one with a statue of Mary, Help of Christians. The pope's boat was anchored between both, and no matter how many ships came to destroy it or how rough the waters became, the pope's ship remained safe. This dream became a foundational element for the order of the Salesians, who to this day maintain a devotion to Christ in the Eucharist and to the Virgin Mary.

St. Francis of Assisi (1182–1226) owed his charism of service to the poor to a vision he experienced. After a pilgrimage to Rome, where he was begging with the poor, he had a mystical vision of a crucified Jesus in the country chapel of San Damiano, in which the Icon of Christ Crucified said to him, "Francis, Francis, go and repair my house, which, as you can see, is falling into ruins." Thinking this referred to the church building he was praying in, Francis sold some cloth from his father's store to assist the priest there for the rehabilitation of the church building. Later he continued his life of personal poverty and service to the poor.

More frequent and more commonly investigated for authenticity by Church authorities, however, are claims of the appearance of heavenly visitors — Christ, the Virgin Mary, saints, and angels — perceivable by the eyes. Marian apparitions are the most common type of vision throughout history; as mentioned earlier, the University of Dayton's International Marian Research Institute reports the occurrence of more than 2,500 claims over the ages. Reports of visions of the Virgin may cause problems for those who question her power and role in making such interventions in human history, but the scriptural basis for the role of Mary cannot be ignored:

- God the Father sent Christ to us physically through Mary.
- At her request, Jesus performed his first miracle — at the Wedding Feast at Cana — and began his public ministry. *("O woman, what have you to do with me? My hour has not yet come." — Jn 2:4)*
- Jesus on the Cross both practically and symbolically entrusted her to the care of St. John. *("Behold, your mother!" And from that hour the disciple took her to his own home. — Jn 19:27)*
- Elizabeth received the grace of God through the visit of Mary. *("For behold, when the voice of your greeting came to my ears, the child in my womb leaped for joy." — Lk 1:44)*
- Jesus Christ is the sole mediator between God and man. *("For there is one God, and there is one mediator between God and men, the man Christ Jesus, who gave himself as a ransom for all." — 1 Tim 2:5–6)* St. Paul has no problem with asking the rest of us (including Mary) to be subordinate mediators as he asks us to pray for each other (Rom 1:9; 1 Thess 5:25; 1 Tim 2:1).

The *Catechism* says that Jesus "is the one intercessor with the Father on behalf of all men, especially sinners" (CCC 2634). It also notes that when we pray for each other, it is a "participation in the intercession of Christ" (CCC 2635).

In his document *Tertio Millennio Adveniente,* Pope John Paul II addressed concern over an overemphasis on Marian devotion at the cost of drawing the faithful away from Christ:

> Veneration of [Mary], when properly understood, can in no way take away from "the dignity and efficacy of Christ the one Mediator." Mary in fact constantly points to her Divine Son and she is proposed to all believers as the *model of faith* which is put into practice. (no. 43)

In their pastoral letter on the Blessed Virgin Mary, the United States Bishops in 1973 released a comment on the value of understanding apparitions.

> Authenticated appearances of Mary are "providential happenings [that] serve as reminders of basic Christian themes: such as prayer, penance, and the necessity of the sacraments."[129]

The clear purpose of apparitions and miracles in general is to give people throughout the world hope and to draw them closer to Christ. People of every culture have embraced the attention of the Blessed Mother, who comes to her children during their times of greatest distress when war, famine, and apostasy have ravaged civilization. She has reached out to the various cultures of the world in a way that only a mother could, adapting to the needs of her varied children by showing herself in the physical traits, dress, and language that would best be received by the recipients of her messages.

Because Marian apparitions almost universally occur in the same place over and over again, the associated Marian titles are named for the place in which they occur — Our Lady of Knock

(Ireland) and Our Lady of Lourdes (France) are famous examples. For others, the sobriquets are derived from the messages or other attributions of the apparition, such as Our Lady of Peace, Our Lady of the Miraculous Medal, and Our Lady with the Golden Heart. Some titles have two variations referring to the same event: Our Lady of the Rosary is the name given to Our Lady of Fátima.

Some of the common elements of Marian apparitions that often attract attention and stir controversy are the prophecies and secrets they often contain. In what is generally considered the greatest Church-approved modern vision, the Virgin Mary was reported to have visited three shepherd children beginning on May 13, 1917, in the Cova da Iria area of Fátima, Portugal, and three prophetic secrets were given to the children and to the world. On May 13, 2000, Cardinal Ratzinger provided a theological commentary specifically on the third secret of Fátima that contained some general insights on how the faithful might approach the miraculous. In quoting 1 Thessalonians 5:19–21, he encouraged proper discernment: "Do not quench the Spirit, do not despise prophesying, but test everything; hold fast what is good." He reminded Catholics about how to approach prophecy:

> In every age the Church has received the charism of prophecy, which must be scrutinized but not scorned. On this point, it should be kept in mind that prophecy in the biblical sense does not mean to predict the future but to explain the Will of God for the present, and therefore show the right path to take for the future.[130]

It is important to remember as well that the recipients and relators of prophecy are human and see things through their personal lens. In his classic book on discerning private revelations, *A Still, Small Voice*, Fr. Benedict Groeschel quotes a Latin proverb to explain why the personal understandings and cultural experiences of the "prophet" creep into the prophecies given to him by God: "That which is received is received in the manner of the receiver."[131]

Some apparitions are renowned for their prophecies and predictions of the future. One dramatic example of this was in the apparitions of the Mother of the Word in Kibeho, Rwanda (1981–1989). The visions began on November 28, 1981, when six young girls and one boy claimed to have seen the Blessed Virgin Mary and Jesus. In the dining room of the children's school, Alphonsine Mumureke asked the vision: "Who are you?" The reply was: "I am the Mother of the Word. I have come to calm you because I have heard your prayers. I would like your friends to have faith, because they do not believe strongly enough." The eight-year apparition is now considered a prophecy of the ethnic genocide that would take place in the country thirteen years later. Tragically, in 1994, visionary Marie Claire became one of its victims. In 1982, a medical commission was appointed, and later a theological one, to investigate the reports. During Mass on June 29, 2001, Bishop Augustin Misago presented his declaration on the authenticity of the apparitions. In April 2014, in a further display of approval, Pope Francis urged the Rwandan bishops to be agents of reconciliation, commending them to the Marian apparition at Kibeho.

Some of the most controversial of approved apparitions were those received by Ida Peederman. In a series of fifty-six apparitions lasting fourteen years, she received many prophecies from the Lady of All Nations, along with a prayer and an image of the Blessed Mother standing on a globe with a cross behind her. The visions included a bevy of geopolitical predictions, which some analysts have deemed to be spot-on. Two weeks after Pope

Pius XII proclaimed the dogma of the Assumption, the apparition identified herself as "the Lady [or Mother] of All Nations," and Ida received details about Mary as "Co-Redemptrix, Mediatrix, and Advocate." Ida was told that this would be the "last and greatest Marian dogma." After some controversy over the prayer to the Virgin, which referenced her as she who "was once Mary" (a phrase that the Congregation for the Doctrine of the Faith later removed from the prayer), and after a series of bishops had looked at the events unfavorably, the appearances were declared supernatural by the local ordinary in 2002.

Other apparitions have featured secrets revealed to the visionaries. The most well-known case of this is, of course, that of Our Lady of Fátima in Portugal in 1917. While tending sheep in a field called the Cova de Iria, ten-year-old Lucia de Santos and her two younger cousins, Francisco and Jacinta Marto, reported six apparitions of Mary, who identified herself as Our Lady of the Rosary. Mary urged praying of the Rosary, penance for the conversion of sinners, and the consecration of Russia to her Immaculate Heart. On October 13, the well-documented great sun miracle of Fátima occurred: thousands of gathered onlookers witnessed the sun dance and descend on them, drying the land previously covered with rain puddles.

The Virgin gave the children three secrets, the third of which was read at the request of Pope John Paul II by Cardinal Angelo Sodano, Secretary of State, on May 13, 2000, with Sr. Lucia in attendance. It related an assassination of a "bishop in white." John Paul II, after his assassination attempt by Mehmet Ali Ağca, which happened in St. Peter's Square on May 13, 1981 (the feast of Our Lady of Fátima), believed that the secret applied to that event. He also beatified the two deceased seers, Jacinta and Francisco, and made the feast day of Our Lady of Fátima universal by ordering it to be included in the Roman Missal.

Other famous approved visions containing secrets are those of Our Lady of La Salette in France in 1846. Six thousand feet up in the French Alps, the Blessed Virgin Mary is believed to have come to eleven-year-old Maximin Giraud and fourteen-year-old Melanie Calvat-Mathieu while they tended sheep. Her appearance in tears of sorrow called for conversion and penance for sins. Maximin and Melanie each received a secret and recorded it for Church officials, who delivered their statement to the bishop. The secrets were rewritten and edited by the seers on multiple occasions, and the contents remain controversial to this day. The most controversial aspect of Melanie's secret, published in 1879, was the statement: "Rome will lose the Faith and become the seat of the Antichrist."[132] Bishop de Bruillard published a pastoral letter in 1851 approving the apparition — but not the secrets — and later in 1879, the completed basilica was consecrated.

The most controversial apparition in the history of the Church has occurred in the small town of Medjugorje in Bosnia–Herzegovina and centers on ten mysterious secrets promised to the six seers who were recipients of daily visions. For more than thirty years, they have continued to report them, although now less frequently. Paramount in the determination of the authenticity of the apparitions is the Virgin's alleged promise of a permanent sign. Since the apparitions began to be reported, more than thirty million pilgrims from all over the world have journeyed to the site. After much scientific testing, the vehement opposition and negative judgment by Ratko Perić, the bishop of Mostar-Duvno, and the Yugoslavian Bishops Commission that rendered a 1991 declaration of the events as not showing proof of supernaturality (though not condemning them), a 2010 Vatican commission was assembled by Pope Benedict XVI. Composed of theologians, psychologists, and Mariologists, the panel of inquiry conducted interviews with the seers and investigated the events and messages. The commission ended on January 18, 2014, and the world awaits the definitive answer. If Medjugorje is eventually approved, it will join but a mere handful of modern occurrences that the Church has deemed worthy of belief. Many miraculous events have come down to us as legendary stories, having occurred in the era prior to the Council of Trent (1545) and before serious scientific investigation was able to verify them. Their approval typically consisted of and resulted from popular acclaim, enduring tradition, and a strong *sensus fidelium*. It wasn't until the beginning of the seventeenth century that apparition claims were more rigorously explored and since that time have demonstrated only a minor fluctuation in their number from century to century. In the twentieth century, those numbers have greatly escalated, causing Joseph Cardinal Ratzinger to term the increase in recent years "a sign of the times."[133]

This selection from St. Louis de Montfort's *True Devotion to the Blessed Virgin* presents the proper position that should be taken toward unapproved Marian devotions and accordingly toward alleged apparitions:

> It is all the more necessary to make the right choice of the true devotion to our Blessed Lady, for now more than ever there are false devotions to her which can easily be mistaken for true ones. The devil, like a counterfeiter and crafty, experienced deceiver, has already misled and ruined many Christians by means of fraudulent devotions to Our Lady.
>
> Day by day he uses his diabolical experience to lead many more to their doom, fooling them, lulling them to sleep in sin and assuring them that a few prayers, even badly said, and a few exterior practices inspired by himself, are authentic devotions.

A counterfeiter usually makes coins only of gold or silver, rarely of other metals, because the latter would not be worth the trouble. Similarly, the devil leaves other devotions alone and counterfeits mostly those directed to Jesus and Mary.... It is therefore very important, first to recognize false devotions to our Blessed Lady so as to avoid them, and to recognize true devotion in order to practice it. (90–91)

In most Marian apparitions, Our Lady seems to select a small number of visionaries and leaves a series of messages with them. In Zeitun, Egypt, in the 1960s, something very different happened: Our Lady reportedly appeared silently hovering above St. Mark's Coptic Church, visible to many people for a span of three years. Our Lady appeared on many occasions, especially at night, and sometimes was accompanied by white doves that would fly around her. These occurrences took place two or three times a week and attracted large crowds by night, sometimes up to 250,000 people. Christians, Jews, Muslims, and unbelievers gathered to view the sight. The apparitions were photographed, filmed, and broadcast on Egyptian TV. An estimated forty million people witnessed the events. Both the Coptic and Roman Catholic Churches approved the apparitions.

In a more famous occurrence, during a pouring rain in the small town of Knock in County Mayo, Ireland, the figures of Mary, Joseph, John the Evangelist, and a lamb representing Christ on a plain altar appeared over the gable of the village chapel, enveloped in a bright light. There were no messages associated with this vision that fifteen people, between the ages of five and seventy-five, witnessed over the course of hours. Investigative commissions were established in 1879 and 1936, and both returned positive verdicts. In 1979 Pope John Paul II visited the shrine for the hundredth anniversary of the apparitions and was joined by more than 450,000 people who came to Knock on that day. On that occasion, he presented a golden rose, a seldom-bestowed token of papal honor and recognition. The feast of Our Lady of Knock is celebrated on August 21.

A couple of times in the Church-approved apparitions of Betania, Venezuela, both the visionary, mystic Maria Esperanza de Bianchini (1928–2004), and a crowd with her saw the Virgin Mary. On March 25, 1984, more than a hundred people saw the Virgin as "the Reconciler of All Peoples and Nations." Matching testimony was provided by all people present: children, adults, doctors, lawyers, and atheists. In 2010, Bishop Paul Bootkoski, ordinary of the Diocese of Metuchen, New Jersey, opened her cause for beatification and canonization, as she had died there in 2004.

Just as the locations and circumstances in which an apparition occurs are extremely varied, the visionaries themselves who witness the Virgin Mary and receive her message are all very different. There is truly no such thing as a typical visionary. Although far less common, apparitions have even been received by nonbelievers. One of the great conversion stories in the history of Catholicism belongs to Marie Alphonse Ratisbonne, an anti-Catholic Jew who befriended a baron during his travels in Rome. The baron, a devout Catholic, challenged him in a bet, so Ratisbonne began wearing the Miraculous Medal as a simple proof of the ineffectiveness of the medal. On January 20, 1842, while waiting for the baron in the church Sant'Andrea delle Fratte, Ratisbonne encountered a vision of Our Lady of the Miracle and soon after converted to Catholicism. He later became a priest and established a religious community devoted to the conversion of the Jews. The following month, the Vatican held a canonical investigation and, after many depositions, it concluded that his sudden conversion was entirely miraculous; an act of God wrought through the powerful intercession of the Virgin.

In the strange case of the apparition of the Virgin of the Revelation in Tre Fontane, Italy, in 1947, the visionary was actually a virulent anti-Catholic who was on his way to carry out an assassination plot on the pope on the very day of the appearance. Bruno Cornacchiola was a poor tram conductor who on April 12 encountered the Virgin for eighty minutes in a grotto at Tre Fontane. Bruno reported that the "beautiful woman," whom his children first saw, had a motherly but sad expression. She wore a green mantle over a white dress with a rose-colored sash around her waist. She held an ash-gray book close to her breast, and at her feet was a crucifix, which had been smashed, on top of a black cloth. Although quickly approved for faith expression in 1947, there has been no definitive judgment about the authenticity of the events.

At the other extreme, there have been apparitions reported by popes, who, as the highest authority in judging apparition claims, by definition experienced "approved" visions of the Virgin Mary. Popes who reported such an event include:

Liberius (356)
St. John I (526)
Honorius III (1227)
Honorius IV (1210–1287)
St. Celestine V (1215–1296)
John XXII (1245–1334)
Callisto III (1378–1458)

Likewise, apparitions have played a role in the lives of many great saints throughout the history of the Church. Several hundred saints have claimed to witness apparitions of Our Lord, the Virgin Mary, or other saints. Fr. René Laurentin's *Dictionary of Marian Apparitions* lists 308 saints with such an honor.

Some of these saints were inspired by the Virgin and used the story of the apparition as a foundational moment both in the promotion and approval of new religious orders. A number of religious orders have their roots in their founders' claiming a Marian apparition as the source of the inspiration:

Although many great saints recognizable to most Catholics and even to those outside the Church were the recipients of apparitions, there are other saints who are known to the world *only* because of having received a holy vision. Many of them were simple people who worked the land or tended farm animals or were cloistered in religious communities. Such visionaries who went from no-names to notables are:

St. Peter Nolasco (Spain, 1218)
St. Simon Stock (England, 1251)
St. Juan Diego (Mexico, 1531)
St. Mariana de Jesus (Quito, Ecuador, 1594)
St. Catherine Labouré (Paris, France, 1830)
St. Bernadette Soubirous (Lourdes, France, 1858)
Bl. Francisco and Bl. Jacinta Marto (Fátima, Portugal, 1917)

If it weren't for their reported apparitions, they might still have lived lives of heroic virtue and been given an eternal reward, but it is safe to say that they would not be formally recognized in the canon of saints of the Catholic Church.

When a saint is canonized, all of his or her words and writings (including mystical ones) have been examined by the Church. The formal recognition of the saint's life of heroic virtue in the form of a beatification or canonization does not, however, imply that the Church officially recognizes the supernaturality of the saint's claims — it merely states that any private revelations that he or she claims are not in conflict with the faith and morals of the Church. There are many saints who had mystical writings or experiences that never were verified on their own merits for being supernatural. Such renowned individuals with unapproved apparition claims include:

Bl. Anne Catherine Emmerich (Germany, 1790)
St. John Vianney (Italy, 1859)
St. Maximilian Kolbe (Poland, 1904)
St. Pio of Pietrelcina (Italy, 1918)

There is neither a typical apparition nor a typical visionary. In consideration of seventeen apparitions with some form of Vatican recognition since Our Lady of Guadalupe in 1531, most visionaries are younger than twenty, with the extreme data outlier being St. Juan Diego, who was fifty-seven at the time of the great event. In the golden era of Marian apparitions (1846–1933), most occurred to a small group of visionaries. In earlier ages, apparitions were more typically experienced by a single individual. It is worth noting that since 1950, there have been five apparitions approved by the local bishop (but not yet formally recognized by the Vatican) that feature singular visionaries with an average age of forty-five. As with other types of mystical phenomena, most approved Marian apparitions have been claimed by women. Figure 5 on the following page gives a breakdown of age and gender of visionaries in Vatican-recognized apparitions.

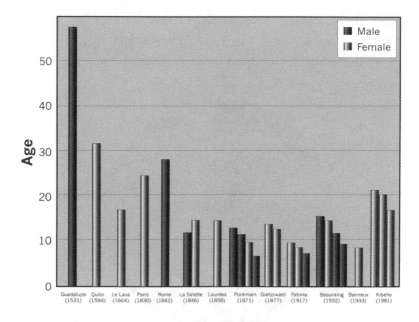

Figure 5.
Age and Gender of Marian Visionaries in
Vatican-Recognized Apparitions

Some visionaries, including notable ones, have gone on to a religious vocation afterward. These include St. Catherine Labouré, Alphonse Ratisbonne, St. Bernadette Soubirous, and Lucia of Fátima. Others, such as Bl. Mariana de Jesus, the visionary of Our Lady of Good Help, had previously entered religious life.

A mystical experience does not guarantee or require a resulting vocation, however. Only ten of the fifty-seven visionaries (see figure 6 on page 136) from the list of the bishop-investigated and approved apparitions entered a religious community. Most modern visionaries of apparitions that have been approved by their local bishop have not entered religious life. These include Maria

Esperanza (Betania,Venezuela), Bernardo Martinez (Cuapa, Nicaragua), Gladys Quiroga (San Nicolás, Argentina), Edson Glauber
(Itapiranga, Brazil), and the children in Kibeho, Rwanda.

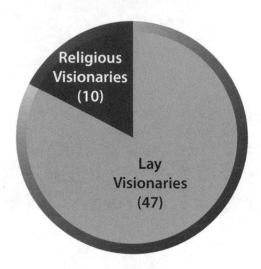

Figure 6.
Lay versus Religious Visionaries in Bishop-Approved Apparitions

The visionaries also have vastly different experiences, especially regarding the duration of the apparitions and the time span
over which they occur. In some instances, such as the group apparitions at Knock and La Salette and the single-visionary apparitions at Pontmain, France, and Alphonse Ratisbonne's experience in Rome in 1842, the visionaries encountered the Virgin on
one occasion. French shepherdess Benedicta Rencurel, however,
received thousands of apparitions of the Virgin from 1664 until
she died in 1718. The Blessed Mother had asked her for a church
and a house for priests to be built, with the intention of drawing
people to greater conversion, especially through the Sacrament of

Penance. The visions accorded to one of history's great mystics, St. Birgitta of Sweden, likewise occurred in the thousands and lasted for many years of her life. One of the aspects that many observers and skeptics of the alleged apparitions at Medjugorje find outlandish and improbable is that the seers reported thousands of messages over thirty years.

VISIONS OF JESUS

In addition to the many apparitions of the Virgin Mary, there have been a few visions of Christ recognized by the Catholic Church as authentic. The Sacred Heart of Jesus is one of Catholicism's most famous and popular devotions. It stems from the reports of the four apparitions of Jesus to St. Margaret Mary Alacoque (1647–1690), a nun from Paray-le-Monial, in Burgundy, France, from 1673 to 1675. Jesus showed his heart to demonstrate the greatness of his love, and he asked St. Margaret Mary to spread the devotion to many people. In 1794, Pope Pius VI praised devotion to the Sacred Heart in his papal bull *Auctorem Fidei*. In 1899, Pope Leo XIII, in his encyclical *Annum Sacrum,* called for the consecration of every person to the Sacred Heart, and on June 11, 1899, he performed the consecration. It was important in historical context to help with the rebirth of Catholicism in Europe, which had fallen to Jansenism and Calvinism.[134]

One of the most popular practices of piety of the modern Church, the Divine Mercy devotion, originated in the apparitions of Jesus to St. Faustina Kowalska. The Polish nun reported a number of apparitions, visions, and conversations with Jesus, which she wrote phonetically in her diary, later published as *Diary: Divine Mercy in My Soul.* The Divine Mercy devotion calls us to ask for and obtain the mercy of God, to trust in Christ's abundant mercy, and to show mercy to others.

Faustina was given the mandate to create an image of Christ: "Paint an image according to the pattern you see with the signature: Jesus, I trust in You.... I promise that the soul that will venerate this image will not perish." Faustina worked directly with an artist from Lithuania to create an image depicting red and pale white rays of light emanating from Jesus' heart; these symbolize the blood and water that flowed from Christ's pierced side (Jn 19:34). The Chaplet of Divine Mercy, which can be prayed on the beads of a standard rosary, became the prayer associated with Divine Mercy with the instruction to pray it at 3 p.m., "the hour of Mercy."

The mystical writings of Faustina were originally suppressed, due to a bad translation, but her memory was later vindicated when she was canonized on April 30, 2000, by John Paul II and is venerated in the Church as the Apostle of Divine Mercy. The first Sunday after Easter was later established by Pope John Paul II as Divine Mercy Sunday and became a great devotion of his, as evidenced by his being canonized on that feast, on April 27, 2014, alongside Pope John XXIII.

CHAPTER 9

Locutions

U nlike the phenomenon of apparitions, in which the visionary reports messages emanating from a physical manifestation of the person of Jesus, the Virgin Mary, or a saint, some
people have claimed a different sort of revelation, in which they
hear audible voices without seeing anything. In some cases, the
words are presented to the recipient as a dictation, but for others,
such as the great saint and patroness of Europe Birgitta of Sweden, knowledge was infused instantaneously. Known as locutions,
these are perhaps the most difficult miraculous phenomenon to
discern, both for the locutionist — the receiver of the divine
messages — and for the Church.

The person hearing the words must ensure that he or she is
not responding to an overactive, pious imagination and be able to
distinguish between those things contemplated in prayer and a direct communication from God. The Church must decide whether it is dealing with a case of mental illness or fraud, as there is
only the testimony and reputation of the locutionist to go on. As
with messages from authenticated visions, pastoral decisions must
be made regarding what to do with the content of these divine
communications.

The idea of God's speaking directly to his people is not a
new one, of course, and instances of hearing a divine voice can be
found throughout the Scriptures.

In Hebrews 1:1–4, Paul tells us of God's speaking to his people: "In many and various ways God spoke of old to our fathers by the prophets." Abraham, Moses, Enoch, Jacob, and others all heard the voice of God. In the very first book of the Bible, God speaks with Adam and Eve:

> And God blessed them, and God said to them, "Be fruitful and multiply, and fill the earth and subdue it; and have dominion over the fish of the sea and over the birds of the air and over every living thing that moves upon the earth." (Gen 1:28)

In the New Testament, at Jesus' baptism by John the Baptist, God the Father speaks to the crowds: "A voice came from the heavens, saying, 'This is my beloved Son, with whom I am well pleased'" (Mt 3:17). Similarly, at the Transfiguration of Christ, after the apparition of Moses and Elijah, Peter, James, and John heard the voice of God: "He was still speaking, when behold, a bright cloud overshadowed them, and a voice from the cloud said, 'This is my beloved Son, with whom I am well pleased; listen to him'" (Mt 17:5). The audible voice of God the Father is heard once again as Jesus speaks of the hour of his glorification:

> "Now is my soul troubled. And what shall I say? 'Father, save me from this hour'? No, for this purpose I have come to this hour. Father, glorify your name." Then a voice came from heaven, "I have glorified it, and I will glorify it again." The crowd standing by heard it and said that it had thundered. Others said, "An angel has spoken to him." Jesus answered, "This voice has come for your sake, not for mine. Now is the judgment of this world, now shall the ruler of this world be cast out; and I, when I

am lifted up from the earth, will draw all men to myself."
(Jn 12:27–32)

Whereas most locutions claimed in modern times tend to have Jesus or the Virgin Mary as their alleged source, Mother Eugenia Elisabetta Ravasio (1907–1990), an Italian nun and mystic known for social work on the Ivory Coast, claimed to have received an apparition and messages from God the Father that have been compiled in the book *The Father Speaks to His Children*. Bishop Alexander Caillot of Grenoble, who was mentioned in the messages, recognized these locutions as supernatural[135] after ten years of examination, making these the only reported private revelation from God the Father that have been approved as supernatural by a bishop. The Vatican has not commented on the divine origin of these messages, but in 1988 an imprimatur was granted by Cardinal Petrus Canisius van Lierde, vicar general for the Vatican City State.[136]

Throughout the history of the Church, many saints and others have claimed to hear voices from heaven. While making her first Communion, Teresa de Jesús "de los Andes" (1900–1920) received from God the mystical grace of interior locutions, which from then on supported her throughout her life. Four years later, another revelation directed her how to live her life: she was to be a Carmelite and seek holiness.[137]

St. Faustina reported having visions of Jesus and conversations with him,[138] which she wrote about in her *Diary*. Her writings were initially suppressed by Church authorities. But eventually Divine Mercy became one of Catholicism's most popular devotions, as Pope St. John Paul II canonized St. Faustina and established a feast day for Divine Mercy.

In her official Vatican biography, the source of inspiration for charitable work at the center of the life of Mother Teresa of

Calcutta (1910–1997) is revealed to be a locution received on September 10, 1946, during a train ride from Calcutta to Darjeeling for her annual retreat.

> On that day, in a way she would never explain, Jesus' thirst for love and for souls took hold of her heart and the desire to satiate His thirst became the driving force of her life. Over the course of the next weeks and months, by means of interior locutions and visions, Jesus revealed to her the desire of His heart for "victims of love" who would "radiate His love on souls." "Come be My light," He begged her. "I cannot go alone." He revealed His pain at the neglect of the poor, His sorrow at their ignorance of Him and His longing for their love. He asked Mother Teresa to establish a religious community, Missionaries of Charity, dedicated to the service of the poorest of the poor.[139]

Some locutions have been claimed to emanate from an icon or a statue. St. Henry of Coquet, a Danish hermit who lived on an island off the British coast, was said to have heard the voice of Christ after meditating on a crucifix:

> After some years a party of Danes tried to persuade him to return to his own country, where there was no lack of site suitable for hermits. But after a night in prayer and experience of a locution from the figure of Christ crucified, he decided to stay on. As his holiness became known, visitors became numerous, attracted by his special gifts of prophesy, telekinesis and reading the secrets of hearts.[140]

Christian devotional history is replete with stories of miraculous Marian images through which a message is conveyed to the faithful. The Orthodox "Quick to Hear" Icon from Mount Athos in Greece gets its name from such an account. St. Neophytos (1134–1214) is said to have had an image of the Theotokos (Mother of God) painted on a Docheiriou monastery wall in the twelfth century. The image resided in obscurity with the monks for more than five hundred years. In 1664, as the refectory steward, Nilos, walked by the image while carrying a lighted torch, a voice said, "Stop dirtying my icon with your smoke." Nilos disregarded the comment, taking it for a prank, and continued on. But then he suddenly lost his sight. Finally after begging pardon, the voice came again: "Monk, your prayer to me has been heard; be forgiven and receive your sight as before…. From now on let the monks fly to me for their every need, and at once I will listen to them and to all who approach me, for I am called Quick to Hear."[141]

Of St. Mary of Egypt (ca. 344–ca. 421), the patron saint of penitents, the *Oxford Dictionary of Saints* relates another such encounter:

Once at Jerusalem, she was held back from entering the church with the other pilgrims by an invisible and irresistible force. Lifting her eyes to an icon of the Blessed Virgin, she was told to go over the Jordan where she would find rest.[142]

In 1973 in Akita, Japan, Sr. Agnes Sasagawa experienced a series of phenomena, including a healing from deafness, the stigmata, and a bleeding and weeping wooden statue of the Virgin Mary that was investigated and received a positive judgment from the local bishop. She also reported receiving locutions from the Virgin Mary through the statue, controversially predicting great troubles in the future of the Church with "bishop against bishop, cardinal against cardinal," and painting an apocalyptic picture of a great tsunami decimating the earth's population.

Locutions have not only affected the Church but have changed the course of human history. The revelations accorded to mystic St. Birgitta of Sweden were considered at the Councils of Constance (1414–1418) and Basel (1431–1449). In 1436, the orthodoxy of the revelations was confirmed. St. Birgitta had received hundreds of locutions on a wide range of topics, including tips for doing laundry, calls for reform in the Church and Sweden, and even the Crusades. In 2010, Pope Benedict XVI in a general audience issued a reminder of the value of St. Birgitta's revelations, as noted by John Paul II in the letter *Spes Aedificandi*:

> "Yet there is no doubt that the Church," wrote my beloved predecessor, "which recognized [Birgitta's] holiness without ever pronouncing on her individual revelations, has accepted the overall authenticity of her interior experience."[143]

The most famous locutions ever claimed were those of St. Joan of Arc (1412–1431). The Maid of Orléans said that she received messages from the Archangel Michael, St. Margaret, and St. Catherine instructing her to support Charles VII and recover France from the English in the Hundred Years' War. Her involvement in the successful siege of Orléans and other swift victories led to Charles VII's coronation at Reims. After her capture, imprisonment, and trial, Joan was declared guilty of heresy and burned at the stake at age nineteen. Twenty-five years after her execution, an examination of the facts ordered by Pope Callixtus

III affirmed her innocence, reversed the charges against her, and declared her a martyr.

Claims of locutions have generated large followings among the faithful. The most popular modern alleged locutions have been those reported by Fr. Stefano Gobbi (1930–2011), an Italian priest who founded the Marian Movement of Priests (MMP), a private association of Catholic clergy and lay associate members, following an interior locution from the Virgin Mary that he claimed to have received in 1972 at the shrine of Our Lady of Fátima.[144] The title of his spiritual diary containing the locutions was changed (although not at the behest of the CDF) from *Our Lady Speaks to Her Beloved Priests* to *To the Priests, Our Lady's Beloved Sons*, so as not to imply the certain authenticity of the messages.

Although the MMP continues to thrive as an organization, the locutions have never been approved by the Church as authentic, nor have they been condemned. As of the year 2000, MMP membership in the United States had reached sixty-three thousand, including four thousand members of the clergy — bishops, priests, and deacons.[145]

In 2012, an alleged mystic popularly known as Maria Divine Mercy (Mary Carberry of Ireland) posted on her website a prophecy that Pope Benedict XVI would be ousted from the Holy See of Rome. When the Vatican announced his retirement on February 11, 2013, Maria Divine Mercy became an instant Internet sensation among supernaturally minded Catholics and conspiracy theorists. She sold her writings in her *Book of Truth* and promoted her messages on her popular website and social media pages, which are followed by hundreds of thousands of interested believers.[146]

As intriguing as such a seemingly accurate prediction might sound, Maria Divine Mercy showed herself to be inspired by the

St. Malachy prophecy of the popes (which identifies the total number of remaining popes and identifies them symbolically), declaring the next *true* pope to be "Peter the Roman." Her prognostication lost all credibility when she asserted that Peter the Roman will be the *actual, historical* St. Peter and that he will reign not on earth but from heaven, until the Second Coming, when he will begin to rule on earth.[147] Calling herself "the 7th Messenger, the 7th Angel," she released other messages containing strange and inaccurate predictions with dates about the end times and the Second Coming of Christ.[148] In a statement from the Archdiocese of Dublin, Archbishop Diarmuid Martin communicated that the "messages and alleged visions have no ecclesiastical approval and many of the texts are in contradiction with Catholic theology."[149]

Due to the popularity of some alleged seers, the Church has responded by providing guidance on these matters. While most alleged apparition or locution cases are handled only by the local bishop, in some rare instances, the Vatican's Congregation for the Doctrine of the Faith (CDF) will intervene. Alleged mystic Vassula Ryden claimed that in November 1985, while writing a mundane list of household items, her hand became stiff and was guided supernaturally to write messages from an angel named Daniel. She later claimed that three months after the initial takeover of her writing, she began to experience visions and messages from Christ and later compiled two thousand such messages into her book *True Life in God*.

In 1995, the CDF published a notification[150] on the writings of Ryden, establishing her writings as not supernatural in origin and restricting her from promoting her messages. According to the CDF analysis, her writings contained "a number of basic elements that must be considered negative in the light of Catholic doctrine" as well as "several doctrinal errors." Another document released in 1996[151] confirmed that the original judgment was still in full force.

In 2007, Cardinal William Levada confirmed that the 1995 notification was still in effect and advised the faithful not to participate in Ryden's activities, including prayer groups. The Greek Orthodox Church and the Church of Cyprus[152] also gave negative judgments against her writings. With additional opposition to her conferences coming from the Scottish Bishops[153] and the Archdiocese of Los Angeles,[154] foremost Mariologist Fr. René Laurentin stated that "she has excited more opposition than any other."[155]

One of the most controversial works of private revelation ever to catch the attention of the Vatican is the 1956 book *The Poem of the Man-God*, a multivolume compilation of about five thousand pages on the life of Jesus Christ written by Italian Maria Valtorta. A Franciscan tertiary and a lay member of the Servants of Mary, Valtorta reported locutions from Jesus Christ since Good Friday, April 23, 1943. Until 1947, she reported visions of Jesus and the Virgin Mary and claimed personal conversations with Jesus that she recorded in more than fifteen thousand handwritten pages as notes extending the stories of the Gospels. The Vatican forbade publication and later placed the book on the Index of Forbidden Books on the instructions of Pope John XXIII. Since the abrogation of the Index in 1965, at the order of the CDF, new publications of the book include a note that the writings do not pertain to supernatural revelations but reflect the author's literary narration of the life of Jesus. *The Poem of the Man-God* has remained controversial, but the work received an imprimatur from Bishop Roman Danylak in 2002.

Two controversial locution cases in the twenty-first century have received an imprimatur from the competent local ordinary and, like most locution claims while the locutionist is alive and the messages go on, have not been established as being supernatural in origin. Catalina "Katya" Rivas, a housewife from Cochabamba, Bolivia, has claimed the stigmata and reported messages from heaven that received the imprimatur of her bishop, René Fernández Apaza, but has been met with much skepticism. A second locutionist, Kathryn Ann Clarke (known as "Anne, a Lay apostle" or "Anne of the Volumes"), living in Illinois and Ireland, began to record her locutions in several volumes titled *Direction for Our Times* after a 2001 visit to Medjugorje. In 2006 and 2011, her writings received an imprimatur from Leo O'Reilly, bishop of the Diocese of Kilmore, Ireland, and were placed under investigation in 2009.[156] As with many claims of private revelation, the authenticity of these messages has been controverted.

CHAPTER 10

Miraculous Images

Throughout Christian history in countries all over the world, images of Jesus and the Virgin Mary have been the source of inspiration and great miracles authenticated by Church authorities, including popes. Miraculous images come in many variations, including bleeding or weeping statues, animated icons, effigies discovered through miraculous means — often at the instruction of the Virgin Mary in an apparition — and images that are said not to be made by human hands. Some have been credited with saving towns from fire, earthquake, famine, and other calamities. Others are simply the objects of great devotion, at whose shrines miracles are worked for the many faithful who gather with their intentions.

Some miraculous images do not boast prodigious origins but have simply become a destination for pilgrimage and an object of great devotion for a specific country, region, or community. The most famous Marian image in one of the most Catholic countries in the world, the great scarred Black Madonna of Our Lady of Czestochowa, also known as Jasna Gora, has become a true symbol of Poland. The image is greatly renowned for having wrought many miracles for the Polish faithful. In 1931, Pope Pius XI established August 26 as the feast day of Our Lady of Czestochowa, and Pope John Paul II visited the shrine four times.

When Spaniards founded the oldest city in the United States, St. Augustine, Florida, in 1565, they brought with them from Madrid a statue of Nuestra Señora de la Leche (Our Lady of the

Milk) in the style of the Virgo Lactans (the Breastfeeding Virgin). In 1765, this statue, along with other religious articles, was lost at sea when England took Spanish Florida for its own colony. When the Spaniards returned in 1783, the devotion to Our Lady under this title flourished. In 1938, a second copy of the original statue in Spain was created in its place. The oldest Marian devotion of the United States has proven to be a powerful one, as people from all over the United States go each year to take part in the statue's procession and to visit the shrine. Many miracles have been reported, especially from couples struggling with infertility who seek Our Lady's assistance and later are blessed with children.

An analysis of the thousands of Marian apparition claims throughout history reveals that the most common message or command that she gives the visionaries is to build her a chapel on that spot. Often a statue of the Virgin miraculously returns to its found location several times (usually three) or becomes so heavy that it cannot be moved by many men, thus sending a signal that a shrine should be built on the spot to house the image.

Around 1630, a man from Portugal was transporting a statue of the Virgin when his mules stopped on the shores of the Luján River. Although the man lightened the beasts' burden, removing everything but the statue, the mules remained unwilling to budge. He left the statue with a slave, who became its guardian for more than forty years, building a brick chapel for the many pilgrims who came to venerate it. It was later moved to the location where it currently resides. In 1887 a basilica was built on the spot. Among the popes who have honored Our Lady of Luján are Clement XI, Clement XIV, Pius VI, Pius IX, Leo XIII, Pius XI, Pius XII, and John Paul II, who personally bestowed a golden rose on the statue of Our Lady.

Legend says that in Sernancelhe, Portugal, in 1498, a mute girl was herding her flock when she found a statue of the Virgin in the cleft of a rock. She made the statue an object of personal devotion, to the dismay of her mother, who thought the image was a doll and threw it into the fire. The girl shouted and grabbed the unburned image out of the fire. She was cured, but her mother's arm became paralyzed. After they both prayed, the mother regained use of her arm. The priest took the image to the parish church, but it miraculously returned to its original spot three times (both a definitive and common number in many of these stories). A chapel was built on the spot and became a major place of pilgrimage. In 1575, Pope Gregory XIII approved the request of King Sebastian to transfer the shrine to the Society of Jesus.

There have been statues and icons that have great signs associated with the images themselves. Many instances of a bleeding or weeping statue have been investigated and, in rare cases, approved by the Catholic Church. In the 1980s, hundreds of Rosa Mystica statues shed tears of blood in thirty countries around the world. The Church did not render definitive judgment on the phenomena. Most alleged miraculous statues have proven to be naturally explainable (plumbing problems, for example), and others have been the products of elaborate hoaxes.

In 1995 in Civitavecchia, Italy, a city seventy kilometers north of Rome, a five-year-old girl, Jessica Gregori, noticed that the statue of the Virgin Mary in the family garden was weeping tears of blood. The statue, brought from alleged Marian apparition site Medjurgorje, went on to bleed on fourteen occasions over ten years. After a series of scientific tests that showed the blood to be human with male characteristics, a panel of experts declared that the events were not explainable. It was approved by Girolamo Grilli, bishop of Civitavecchia — he had personally removed the statue from storage to display it and witnessed the tears of blood himself.

Perhaps the weeping-statue case with the highest level of ecclesial approval is the Weeping Madonna of Syracuse, Italy. The statue first wept on August 29, 1953, in the home of Antonia and Angelo Iannuso. On that day, Antonia suffered a seizure and became temporarily blind. When her vision returned, she saw tears flowing from a small plaster image of the Virgin that had been given to the Iannusos as a wedding gift. When the tears continued, the Iannusos moved the statue outside their home for the gathering crowds to see. The lacrimation was captured on film and investigated by scientists, who determined that the statue was emitting human tears. The commission examined the smooth finish of the statue and found it to have no pores or irregularities on the surface. The backing was removed, and the unfinished gypsum was scrutinized and found to be dry, even though tears were collecting on the reverse side. Many people who visited the statue claimed miracles — 290 in all, of which 109 were validated. Pope Pius XII later made a declaration on Vatican Radio declaring the Weeping Madonna of Syracuse to be an authentic miracle.

One of the most fascinating cases in history occurred in 1973, when a deaf nun named Sr. Agnes Sasagawa encountered a bright light emanating from the tabernacle in her convent's chapel on several occasions. She saw her guardian angel, and subsequently an illuminated three-foot-high wooden statue of Our Lady of All Nations bled from its hand. During the course of eight years and 101 messages, the statue began to weep as well. Scientific tests showed that they were human tears and blood. Later, Sr. Agnes's hearing was restored permanently, as promised by the angel. After several official inquiries, these events of Akita, Japan (but not the apocalyptic messages concerning natural disasters and Church corruption), were approved as supernatural by the local ordinary, Bishop John Shojiro Ito in 1984.

In June 1988, Bishop Ito brought his pastoral letter to Cardinal Joseph Ratzinger, who allowed its dissemination to the faithful. Akita remains a controversial and often ignored miraculous phenomenon.

One of the more difficult types of miracle claims to believe are those that involve an allegedly moving (usually termed "animated") statue or icon. Throughout the ages, and mostly in medieval times, legends and stories have been passed down about objects of religious art in motion. These events require many trustworthy witnesses with good vision and a sound mind. On the night of April 20, 1906, an oleograph of the Virgin of Sorrows, La Dolorosa del Colegio, hanging in the refectory of the Jesuit College of St. Gabriel, in Quito, Ecuador, began to open and shut its eyes in front of thirty-five boarding students and two monks. The image was moved to the school chapel, where the prodigy recurred six times. After a canonical investigation, Church authorities declared that it was "worthy of belief." The image was canonically crowned on April 22, 1956, during the fiftieth-anniversary celebration.

Notre-Dame-du-Cap (Our Lady of the Cape), the most well-known Canadian title of the Virgin Mary, is famous for two miracles. In 1879, a pastor instructed his congregation to pray the Rosary to obtain ice to cross the river so materials and tools could be brought to the site of the new church. Seemingly miraculously, pieces of ice floated downstream from Lake St. Pierre, forming a "rosary bridge" across the St. Lawrence River allowing the construction of the church. On June 22, 1888, three men praying in the chapel witnessed the eyes of the statue of the Virgin repeatedly open and close. News of the event and the fame of the miraculous image spread. The feast of Notre-Dame-du-Cap is celebrated on August 15.

Other images are key elements in the stories of Marian apparitions. One summer day in 1608 in Siluva, Lithuania, a number of children were playing while tending their sheep in a field on the outskirts of the village. They beheld a beautiful young woman standing on the rock, holding a baby in her arms and weeping bitterly. With the town (and surrounding region) entirely Calvinist by this time, the local pastor stepped forward as a representative of the people and asked the woman why she was crying. In sadness over the loss of the town's Catholic identity, she replied, "There was a time when my beloved Son was worshipped by my people on this very spot. But now they have given this sacred soil over to the plowman and the tiller and to the animals for grazing." And she vanished. A blind man, more than a hundred years old, lived in a nearby village. The story of the apparition reached him, and he recalled a night, some eighty years before, when he helped the Catholic priest at the time to bury an ironclad chest filled with church treasures. The villagers led him to the field of the apparitions to see if he could help locate the place where the treasures were buried. No sooner had he reached the spot than his sight was miraculously restored. Falling to his knees with joy and gratitude, he pointed to the exact spot where the chest had been buried. The chest was dug out of the ground, and when it was opened, there — perfectly preserved — were a large painting of the Madonna and Child, several gold chalices, vestments, church deeds, and other documents. The painting was enshrined permanently in the Basilica of the Birth of the Blessed Virgin Mary and is venerated to this day as the Miraculous Image of Siluva. Faith was restored to the town that had lost its Catholic identity to the Calvinists over the course of eighty years.

According to legend, in 1326 in Cácerces, Extremadura, Spain, the Virgin Mary appeared to a cowherd named Gil Cordero as he searched for a lost cow. The Virgin led him to a mound of stones, where he saw his motionless cow, which appeared dead. Cordero was ready to cut off its hide when suddenly the beast sprang up, stunning him. The Virgin told him to call the local authorities to dig at that very spot. Not believing his story at first, when they dug at the designated spot and removed the stones, they found a cave and inside it a statue with an ancient document explaining its origin. It was the famous wonderworking image that Pope Gregory the Great had sent to Spain eight hundred years earlier. A small church and later a basilica were built, helping to make the devotion to Our Lady of Guadalupe one of the most popular in all of Spain and a favorite Marian title of Columbus himself.

This devotion clearly predates the Mexican one of the same name. The Virgin was also called Our Lady of Guadalupe in Mexico because — according to some explanations — the visionary St. Juan Diego called her "Coātlaxopeuh," meaning in his native Nahuatl "the one who crushes the serpent," and to the Spanish ear of the bishop, that sounded like Guadalupe, a familiar name.

The prodigious image of Our Lady of Guadalupe from Tepeyac Hill in the area of what is now Mexico City belongs to a group of what are perhaps the most fascinating of all miraculous images and even the most fascinating of miracles of any sort. They have been classified as *acheiropoeita* (Greek for "not made by human hands"). In modern times, our thoughts may turn to those things that bring the Catholic Church ridicule, naturally occurring images that the overzealous faithful prop up as signs from heaven. Once or twice a year, a local news station somewhere in the United States will report on a "miraculous" stain or discoloration that people perceive to be the Virgin Mary. These are likely mere pareidolia, the brain's assigning a familiar image to a random pattern (as in psychology with the Rorschach inkblot test) as in the case of the "Grilled Cheese Virgin Mary." A giant colorful image like a blurry Our Lady of Guadalupe appeared in 1996 on an office building in Clearwater, Florida, drawing almost five hundred thousand visitors within weeks. Chicagoans might remember the image of "Our Lady of the Underpass" appearing on the Fullerton Avenue viaduct in the city's Bucktown neighborhood.

Throughout history, there has been only one such "stain" image of the Virgin Mary that has received official recognition from Church authorities as having a supernatural origin. In 1797, in the small village of Absam, near Innsbruck, a young girl named Rosina Buecher was astonished to see an image of the Virgin Mary appear in the windowpane next to her as she prayed for her father's safe return from a mining accident. The glass was scrubbed by investigators and the image disappeared — but then reappeared. Even attempts to remove it permanently with acid failed. The image was considered inexplicable, and both the priest and bishop declared it a miracle. Many healings were claimed. Today, the small glass pane with the image of the Virgin is enshrined in the parish church for veneration.

In the highlands of northeastern Colombia, the people of Ocaña celebrate Our Lady of Graces, whose image appeared more than three hundred years ago beneath the bark of a tree. A mestizo named Cristóbal Melo maintained a nearby sugar mill and small farm, which he worked with his son. In 1709 he went into the mountains to find a log to make a trough. After selecting the wood, Cristóbal removed the bark and saw formed in low relief in the sapwood an image of Our Lady in the form of the Immaculate Conception that became known to be miraculous. The annual fiesta, which attracts pilgrims from a wide area, features Masses, music, and a procession.

In a few cases, an image of Christ's face has been said to appear on a consecrated host as part of a Eucharistic miracle. Another type of Eucharistic miracle has become one of the most well-documented miracles in history. In 1330, during a Mass in Walldurn, Germany, Fr. Heinrich Otto knocked over the chalice containing consecrated wine. The spilled wine immediately changed into physical blood and stained the cloth known as the corporal. What was left behind was a red image of the Crucified Christ, surrounded by eleven identical images of the head of Christ with crowns of thorns. The holy relic was preserved in the Church of St. George in Walldurn, where thousands of pilgrims continue to travel each year to venerate it. Pope Eugene IV confirmed the miracle in 1445 and granted indulgences to pilgrims. Pope John XXIII extended further approval by elevating the church to the status of a minor basilica, now known as the Minor Basilica of St. George and the Most Precious Blood.

Some miraculous images of indeterminate origin have even baffled scientists. In 1754, Maria Mueses de Quiñones, an Indian woman from the village of Potosi, Colombia, and her deaf-mute daughter, Rosa, were caught in a very strong storm. They sought refuge in a cave. To Maria's surprise, her mute daughter exclaimed with her first words, "The mestiza is calling me!" Maria did not see the figures of a woman and child whom the girl described and fearfully ran back with her daughter to Ipiales and told the townspeople. After later returning to the spot, the woman saw an apparition of Our Lady and Child. Some months later, Rosa died and was returned to life when her mother prayed again at the cave. The townspeople went to see the place and encountered a miraculous image burned into the rocks. Testing has shown this lasting image to be of indeterminate origin. "Geologists from Germany bored core samples from several spots in the image. There is no paint, no dye, nor any other pigment on the surface of the rock. The colors are the colors of the rock itself. Even more incredible, the rock is perfectly colored to a depth of several feet!"[157]

The apparitions of Our Lady of Guadalupe to St. Juan Diego (1474–1548) are remembered for the great story of the Virgin appearing on several occasions to the hesitant middle-class worker and requesting that a temple be built at that place in order that her Son might be honored. Juan Diego's attempt to persuade the Spanish bishop-elect to begin this great undertaking was received favorably only when the devout native unfurled his tilma (cloak) and revealed the most famous Marian image ever known. The shrine was built, and almost nine million natives over the next decade were baptized in the wake of these visions. In 1945, Pius XII stated that the Virgin of Guadalupe was the "Queen of Mexico and Empress of the Americas" and that her image was painted "by brushes that were not of this world." In his historic 1979 visit to the Basilica of Our Lady of Guadalupe in Mexico City, Pope John Paul II called her the "Star of Evangelization," knelt before her image, invoked her motherly assistance, and called upon her as Mother of the Americas.

The documentation surrounding these visions is spotty, and the visionary himself, despite being canonized by John Paul II in 2002, does not have much conclusively written about him either. In the first formal inquiry and investigation, named *Informaciones Guadalupana*, from February 18 to March 22, 1666, Juan Diego was called a "holy man." A great oral tradition surrounds these apparition events to supply enough details to assure us of their veracity, but the wondrous image, emblazoned on a cactus-fiber cloak that should have decayed in thirty years, still remains.

To the eyes and understanding of the people of this region at that time, the tilma reads as a *codex*, a collection of Nahuatl symbolics and glyphs on the inside robe that would serve as a catechism of sorts. One glyph in particular, a four-petaled flower, representing the north, south, east, and west (i.e., the one true God, who is everywhere), is found just once on the image, on the pregnant belly of the woman. In addition to being able to see that she is the virginal Mother of God, she is positioned in front of the rays of the sun, indicating that she is greater than the natives' sun god, and standing on the moon, showing her superiority to that god. Despite this positioning, she is also quickly known not to be a god. Her head is bowed, her hands are folded, and her feet are kicked up in a dance step — all indications that she is in prayer.

Other miracles are associated with this image. In addition to being spared the natural course of degradation, the image was not damaged by a nitric-acid spill in 1785 when a worker attempted to clean the frame, nor was it destroyed by a bomb intended to incinerate it that destroyed the marble surrounding it.

One of the great mysteries of the image of Guadalupe is that it has never been determined how it was created. The image on the tilma is composed of pigments that have not been identified by chemical analysis as being the product of animal, vegetable, or mineral dye. Even with the use of X-rays and other analysis technologies, no brushstrokes or undersketch below the painting has been identified.

On May 7, 1979, Philip Serna Callahan, an accomplished biologist who has written fourteen books and two hundred scientific papers, was invited by the rector of the shrine, Msgr. Enrique Salazar, to conduct infrared photographic tests on the tilma. Infrared photography allows the scientist to obtain "historical data of the historical derivation, the method of rendition and the validity of documents and paintings." Between 9 p.m. and midnight, he took forty exposures, from a distance and close up, and concluded that the original image had been substantially embellished over the years. The first additions were the moon and the tassel, followed by the gold and black decorations, the angel, and the fold in robe, the sunburst, and the background. The elements that were found to be original are the red robe, the blue mantle, the face, and the hands. Callahan noted:

> In terms of this infrared study, there is no way to explain either the kind of color pigments, or the maintenance of color luminosity and brightness over the centuries.
>
> When consideration is given to the fact that there is no under drawing, sizing or over varnish, and the weave of the fabric itself is utilized to give the portrait depth, no explanation of the portrait is possible by infrared techniques. It is remarkable that after more than four centuries there is no fading or cracking of the original figure on any portion of the agave tilma, which should have deteriorated centuries ago.[158]

Additional discoveries have added to the image's renown as a great prodigy. Dr. Hernández Illescas, a medical doctor and amateur astronomer working with Fr. Mario Rojas, performed an astronomical study of the star pattern on the tilma and found that the stars on Mary's mantle align with those seen in the Mexican sky at the exact longitude and latitude of Tepeyac Hill in the winter-morning solstice of December 12, 1531, at 10:26 a.m., which corresponds exactly to the date and time traditionally given for the apparition.

Dr. José Aste Tonsmann, a scientist at IBM, used high-resolution photography to magnify the image 2,500 times, brightening it at 25,000 illuminated points per square millimeter, and running noise-reduction filters to enhance the image. He revealed an image of thirteen people in the pupils and corneas of the eyes of the Virgin on the tilma, consistent with the number of people present when the saint revealed the image to the bishop-elect and his attendants. Tonsmann published his findings in 1981 in *El Secreto de Sus Ojos*.

Other discoveries from research on the tilma continue to be unearthed. The tilma has been identified as a topographical map with the glyphs for water and mountains being claimed to align with Mexican geography. Some have successfully translated the symbols of the tilma into a musical composition.[159]

Even with the image of Guadalupe's many wonders, the most widely studied religious artifact in history is the Shroud of Turin, the reputed burial cloth of Christ. The Shroud of Turin, with its brownish image of a tortured man's body lightly tingeing a wide white cloth, has been venerated as a true relic by the faithful for hundreds of years, but skeptics have labeled it a medieval forgery due to a lack of an early written record. When the image was first viewed in the photographic negative in 1898 (and later in 1931), people could finally visualize the person of Christ, and later 3-D scanning techniques further gave depth to the range in contrast.

The relic continues to attract massive crowds when it is placed on public display. From the years 1900 to 2000, the Shroud had been made accessible to pilgrims only five times.[160] For a spring 2015 showing, more than six hundred thousand people signed up to view the Shroud.[161] Numerous popes have venerated it. Following in the footsteps of his predecessors Benedict XVI and John Paul II, who visited the site of the linen burial cloth, Pope Francis, in the first days of his pontificate, referred to the face of the man depicted in the Holy Shroud as "all those faces of men and women marred by a life which does not respect their dignity, by war and violence which afflict the weakest."[162]

Medical specialists have determined that the man on the Shroud exhibits wound patterns consistent with the Gospel accounts of the Passion of Christ. The details of the lashings that Christ received from a Roman flagrum are seen in more than 120 scourge marks found on the image. The piercing of Christ's side, which produced blood and water, is shown by an entry point for a spear and the presence of watered-down blood (i.e., blood with plasma). The blood found on the scalp area of the Shroud image does not correspond to the marks that would have been made by what we commonly visualize as a ring-shaped crown of thorns. The Shroud displays marks all over the head, as if a cap of thorns had been placed on the head.

The blood markings on the cloth present several other mysteries. The blood is human blood (MNS) of the type AB. The color is surprisingly red, instead of brown or black, as would be expected after many centuries. Scientists, however, have identified a prevalence of bilirubin, the breakdown product of red blood cells, which implies the prolonged torture of the man prior to his death, allowing the bilirubin to mix with the man's blood. Inexplicably, the rivulets of blood seen flowing on the image were undisturbed by the body's being removed from the cloth. Underneath each blood clot on the cloth, there is no presence of the image.

An extremely knowledgeable medieval forger would have had to take into account each of these things in producing a forgery of this detail. He would also have had to ignore every depiction of the crucified Christ he had ever seen, as the man on the Shroud has wounds in his wrists instead of in the palms of his hands, because the weight of the human body could not be supported in crucifixion through the hands. Such a piercing through the wrist would result in the piercing of the median nerve, causing the thumb to bend inward. The Shroud image accurately does not display the thumbs of the man. On the feet, there is evidence of one nail wound between the metatarsals, not breaking any bones and coming out the bottom of the foot.

Some Shroud authenticity advocates have claimed to have successfully matched the pollen and bloodstain pattern on the face of the Shroud to the Sudarium of Oviedo.[163] This relic, kept in the Cathedral of San Salvador, Oviedo, Spain, is claimed by some to be the cloth wrapped around the head of Jesus Christ after he died, as mentioned in John 20:6–7. Using a polarized image overlay technique to study the Shroud and the Sudarium, Dr. Alan Whanger, professor emeritus of Duke University, found seventy points of correlation between the two images on the front and fifty on the back.[164] The presence of pollen from Palestine has been identified in studies by Max Frei of Switzerland and others. Other unique pollen samples found on each image support the view that each relic took a different path after leaving Jerusalem.[165]

The Sudarium is considered distinct from any of the many legendary and purportedly miraculous images of the face of Christ, including those called the Veronica Veil, the Mandylion, the Edessa image, or the Manoppello image. Some from this list are no longer extant or never were.

The Vatican has never taken a stance on the validity of the ancient cloth, but in 1978 it invited a high-level, multidisciplinary team of twenty-four scientists from top international institutions to Turin to study it in depth.

The scientists conducted 120 hours of investigative work in which they collected samples that they sent back to the United States for analysis. In 1981, the Shroud of Turin Research Project (STURP), including scientists from Caltech, the United States Air Force Academy, and Los Alamos Labratory, published their findings of the image as scientifically inexplicable:

No pigments, points, dyes or stains have been found on the fibrils. X-ray, fluorescence and microchemistry on the fibrils preclude the possibility of paint being used as a method for creating the image. Ultra Violet and infrared evaluation confirm these studies.[166]

More than one hundred subsequent Shroud studies concurred that the image could not be explained by science.[167] The findings attracted other members of the scientific community, and the focus of investigation went from the nature and source of the image to its age. Skeptics believed that the image dated to the fourteenth century, when it first entered recorded history. In 1988, the process of carbon-14 dating was applied to settle the debate. The test was performed on small samples of cloth from the icon by three laboratories, at the universities of Oxford and Arizona, and the Swiss Federal Institute of Technology, which concurred that the samples they tested dated from the Middle Ages, between 1260 and 1390. The results did nothing to answer how the image was created and instead set off two decades of further debate carried out in the popular press and scientific journals. The scientific community pointed to the highly credentialed scientific team that performed the test in independent laboratories separated around the world, while others had come up with now discredited theories to account for the results being centuries off the mark. The possibility of bacterial contamination of the cloth has been suggested, noting that burial shrouds for Egyptian pharaohs have produced inaccurate test results that are off by centuries.[168]

Still others questioned the way the testing was done. Dr. Wayne Phillips, a medical expert on the Shroud, has called the next development in the history of Shroud examination "miraculous." Unexpectedly in 2001, someone not from the scientific community, a nurse named Sue Benford, released some findings that changed the way scientists began to view the test results. In 1988, merely out of curiosity, she requested copies of images of the entire sample of the Shroud. After spending countless hours looking at the fiber pattern on the images, she identified a mis-alignment in the weave of the material between the edges of the Shroud (where the radiocarbon testing was done) and the central part of the cloth (where the image is located). According to Phillips, when the Shroud was held up for display by clerics over hundreds of years, it was constantly handled and potentially damaged at its outer edges. The scientists who tested the Shroud in 1978 did not examine the corners, but only the image area. A medieval repair job in this location was not out of the question. Without telling anyone that the imagery came from the Shroud, Benford sent the image samples to three independent cloth inspectors to find out whether something was wrong with the cloth, and they all came back with the same result: that the cloth appeared to have been repaired at that location. The original investigators from the STURP team were contacted with these findings. The group's chemist, Ray Rogers, verified that linen (original) and cotton (new addition) end-to-end threads could be identified in a cloth that was known to be 100 percent linen. The leftover materials from the samples used for the 1988 carbon-14 dating were then obtained, and it was determined that it was in fact a patch job of cotton reweaving.

In 2008, these results were published in a major chemistry journal, *Chemistry Today*, stating that the samples provided to the labs were in fact flawed and that the actual age of the Shroud could be much earlier than the testing showed.[169] As a result, new interest in the Shroud has been sparked, and research on image formation, once set aside by the 1988 results, has been reinitiated.

Miracle or great hoax? The debate rages on.

Chapter 11

Eucharistic Miracles

Christianity's greatest miracle is the transubstantiation of the Eucharist that happens daily all over the world. This central dogma of the Catholic Faith boldly claims that despite retaining all the physical characteristics of bread and wine (known as accidents), these food staples, once consecrated, truly become the actual flesh and blood of the Son of God during the Sacrifice of the Mass. Many people have ignored this great event, saying that the bread and wine are mere symbols and that Jesus used them at the Last Supper in an act of commemoration and celebration of community. It would seem like an acceptable and comfortable interpretation of Jesus' intention and ease this strange notion of required cannibalism, but to see that this interpretation is incorrect one has to look no further than the Gospel of John to the scandal that Jesus caused with his command:

> So Jesus said to them, "Truly, truly, I say to you, unless you eat the flesh of the Son of man and drink his blood, you have no life in you; he who eats my flesh and drinks my blood has eternal life, and I will raise him up at the last day. (Jn 6:53–54)

Many of Jesus' followers left him because of this unbelievable and confusing suggestion. Yet he did not clarify his statement or follow with a parable to show the symbolism in his words or chase after all the people who had followed him dutifully up to that point.

Throughout history to this modern day, skeptics and believers alike have likewise questioned and struggled with this core belief. The sheer impossibility of it seems to be matched by the why of it: why would the Creator of the universe humble himself to take the form of a lifeless piece of food, easily ignored and able to be desecrated? The doubt over whether Christ's body, blood, soul, and divinity could be truly present in the Eucharist has caused many to receive this gift when not in good standing with the Catholic Church.

The Catholic Church affirms the Eucharist as the central element of the life of faith:

The Eucharist is the source and summit of all Christian life. In the Eucharist, the sanctifying action of God in our regard and our worship of him reach their high point. It contains the whole spiritual good of the Church, Christ himself, our Pasch. Communion with divine life and unity of the People of God are both expressed and effected by the Eucharist. Through the Eucharistic celebration we are united already with the liturgy of heaven and we have a foretaste of eternal life.[170]

A few times throughout history, this invisible mystery has come to life in a very visible way through Eucharistic miracles. The proof exists for all to see in the hundreds of instances of additional physical phenomena associated with a consecrated host. Many are still displayed in churches around the world. Such evidence has led skeptics to believe in Christ's real presence in the Eucharist.

Eucharistic miracles come in many varieties. Perhaps the most convincing are the cases in which the consecrated wafer, commonly known as the host, has been transformed into human flesh. Other times the Eucharist has been seen to bleed human blood as verified by scientific testing. Other consecrated hosts have been inexplicably preserved for hundreds of years or have fortuitously escaped danger by passing through a fire unscathed or vanishing from the clutches of thieves. Some miraculous stories report the levitation of consecrated hosts. In the hagiographies of saints throughout Church history, holy men and women have experienced great miracles of the Eucharist, including the strange phenomenon of surviving on no food except for the bread consecrated into the body of Christ.

In perhaps the earliest known case of a Eucharistic miracle, generally regarded as the most famous, a Basilian hieromonk of Lanciano, Italy, around the year 700 entertained serious doubts about whether the Eucharist constituted the true flesh and blood of Christ. At the monastery of St. Longinus, after saying the words of consecration ("This is my body.... This is my blood"), a ring of human flesh formed around the wafer, and in the chalice five globules of human blood formed (in correspondence to each of the five wounds traditionally ascribed to Christ at the Crucifixion).[171] This great physical miracle was reserved in a monstrance or ostensorium for future generations to visit in adoration.

The prodigious Eucharist underwent four investigations beginning in 1574 before modern scientists were able to investigate it in 1971. Dr. Odoardo Linoli, professor emeritus in human anatomy at the University of Siena, was assisted by Dr. Ruggero Bertelli, a retired professor of human anatomy, pathological histology, chemistry, and clinical microscopy at the University of Siena. In their findings they determined that there was no trace of preservatives in the flesh, which was determined to be human striated muscular tissue of the heart wall. The blood was also found to be of human origin and of the same type blood type as the flesh, AB. In the blood were found proteins in the same proportions as are found in the seroproteic makeup of fresh normal blood.[172] They also mention in their 1973 report *Quaderni Sclavo di Diagnostica Clinica e di Laboratori* that blood spoils rapidly when taken from a cadaver and only a skilled modern surgeon could have removed the tissue sample, ruling out the possibility of a medieval hoax.

Another instance of the Eucharistic bread physically transforming into human flesh occurred in Regensburg, Germany, in 1194. According to the account, a devout woman received the Eucharist at Mass but removed the host from her mouth and brought home with her so that she might adore it in her home. Some years later, after guilt inspired her to confess her impropriety to the parish priest, he opened the container to find that it had partially turned to human flesh. The bishop investigated the event and displayed the host in a golden monstrance in the cathedral, where it became renowned as the source of healings and other miracles.[173]

There are many Eucharistic miracles throughout history that involve a host that begins to bleed. On Easter Sunday, March 28, 1171, in Ferrara, Italy, in the Basilica of Santa Maria in Vado, Fr. Pietro da Verona broke the consecrated host and saw blood gush forth from it, sprinkling the vaulted ceiling above with small droplets. In 1595, the ceiling was enclosed within a small shrine.[174] Almost two centuries later, in Macerata, another priest with doubts about the Real Presence broke the consecrated host and found blood flowing from it, staining his vestments.[175]

In addition to bleeding hosts, occasionally the consecrated wine has become true blood, as in the seminal Eucharistic miracle at Lanciano. In 1310 in Fiecht, Austria, in the chalice of a doubting priest, Abbot Rupert, the precious blood began to boil and overflow after the Consecration. Many years later, the blood remained as if fresh from a wound and was enshrined there for pilgrims to venerate.[176]

Although most cases of bleeding hosts happen in the monstrance during adoration or during the Consecration at Mass, some modern mystics have claimed to have experienced a bleeding host on their tongues. The Church has not formally approved any of these recent occurrences and in fact has declared the phenomenon "not supernatural" in the case of alleged seer Julia Kim from Naju, Korea,[177] who has claimed a myriad of additional phenomena, including visions, healings, stigmata, and a bleeding statue.[178]

In some Eucharistic miracles the consecrated host miraculously survives conditions that it should not have. On March 12, 1345, Ybrand Dommer, a fisherman from Amsterdam was near death, and the parish priest gave him the last rites. Dommer later vomited up everything he had consumed that day, including the Eucharist, which was hastily thrown into the fire by the maid. The next day, one of the other maids saw a strange light coming from the fire and recovered the perfect host and brought it to the priest. In a common miracle-story detail, the host miraculously returned three times to the man's home, which was turned into a chapel. A hundred years later, its monstrance and the host survived another fire (the chapel did not), adding to the renown of the prodigy. The events are commemorated each year on the eve of Palm Sunday.[179]

From Avignon, France, comes another story of the Eucharist surviving difficult odds. On November 30, 1433, when the river Rodano overflowed and flooded the city, two members of the Gray Penitents confraternity realized that they had left the Eucharist exposed for adoration and that the chapel was being inundated with water. With great difficulty, they rowed a boat to the chapel, where they discovered that the waters inside had parted around the Eucharist, leaving it dry and unharmed. Even today this miracle is celebrated yearly on November 30 with a sacred chant from the Canticle of Moses relating to the parting of the Red Sea.[180]

In 1750, in another story of the Eucharist in peril, the golden ciborium and the many consecrated hosts it contained were stolen from the Basilica of St. Francis in Siena, Italy, while the priests and the faithful were gathered for the vigil of the Feast of the Assumption. The town gathered in prayer for the safe return of the hosts, and perhaps because of a miraculous change of heart, the thieves secretly returned the ciborium out of guilt. The hosts were later discovered stuffed in the poor box of the church, soiled and covered with dust and cobwebs from the box. When the priest discovered this, he cleaned and counted the wafers and found that every stolen piece — 348 whole hosts and 6 halves — had been recovered. Perhaps more miraculously, the hosts have survived to this day in perfect condition, without mold, and have remained fresh as verified by the investigating bishop.[181]

In some rare instances, the host in the monstrance has been claimed to display a holy image on it during adoration. Normally such things are to be considered the products of pious imagination, mass hysteria, or, in the case of an individual witness, pareidolia. Something very different happened in 1822, in Bordeaux, France, in the chapel of Our Lady of Loreto, after Abbot Delort presided over Benediction with the Blessed Sacrament. For more than twenty minutes, a living, moving likeness of Christ — not a simple static image — was witnessed appearing on the host that was being adored. The archbishop of Bordeaux, Msgr. D'Aviau, interviewed the witnesses of the event and declared it worthy of belief.[182]

Another bishop-approved Eucharistic image occurred in modern times. On April 28, 2001, in the Malankara Catholic

Church in Chirattakonam, India, the parish priest and other faithful in adoration noticed several dark spots forming on the consecrated wafer. After reserving it in the tabernacle for the week, the
priest could make out the face of a bearded man that the congregation seemed to notice as well. The image clarified over time to
such a degree that even the local bishop accepted it as miraculous
and prayed for discernment over what the sign could signify for
his congregation.

In addition to the variations in miracles in which the host
manifests inexplicable characteristics or survives treacherous circumstances, there are many stories in the lives of saints of noteworthy Eucharistic phenomena. Many saints experience moments of incredible joy and connection with God — ecstasies
and rapture — at the moment of receiving Communion. Other
stories tell of a host being delivered by angels or appearing out
of thin air on a saint's tongue. Some saints experience visions or
hear voices in conjunction with their reception of the Eucharist.
There are tales of great lights illuminating the Eucharist and saints
witnessing the host rise into the air.

The most common miracle is the Eucharistic fast, otherwise
known as inedia, in which the saint survives only on the Eucharist for physical sustenance. Nutritional science would find this
impossible, as an average adult burns approximately two thousand
calories per day, and although it provides immeasurable spiritual
value, a thin wafer of bread can provide but a single calorie.

One of the great saints of the Catholic Church, Catherine
of Siena (1347–1380) was an Italian nun known for her political
influence, such as convincing Pope Gregory to return to Rome
from Avignon, as well as her mystical gifts. She was said to be
mystically married to Christ, as signified by a ring of hardened
flesh around her finger. Her autobiography claims that she had
the ability to levitate as well as the stigmata, which was kept invis-

ible at her request. In one of the many visions she received eight years before her death, she drank from the blood of Jesus emanating from the wound in his side, after which she subsisted on nothing but the bread of the Eucharist. When asked by her spiritual director about whether she suffered great hunger, she replied, "God satisfies me so in the Holy Eucharist that it is impossible for me to desire any species of corporal nourishment."[183]

One famous case of inedia is that of Portuguese mystic Bl. Alexandrina Maria da Costa (1904–1955), who experienced mystical gifts from a young age. In March 1918, at fourteen years old, to avoid being attacked, she jumped out of a building, resulting in a broken spine and paralysis that confined her to bed from 1925 onward. Her mystical writings revealed her to be a victim soul, uniting her sufferings with Christ's. According to her Vatican biography, from March 1942, for about thirteen years until her death, she received no food except for the Holy Eucharist; this verified by a hospital and by doctors.[184]

The phenomenon of inedia often accompanies the stigmata, the presence of the wounds of Christ. Bl. Anne Catherine Emmerich (d. 1824) received revelations of the life and Passion of Christ, which led to the discovery of Mary's Holy House in Ephesus, and was frail and bedridden for many years while suffering the wounds of Christ. She survived on water and the Holy Eucharist for the last twelve years of her life.

Another German mystic, Therese Neumann (1898–1962), whose beatification cause was opened by Bishop Gerhard Muller in 2005, is an example of a person surrounded by a myriad of inexplicable physical maladies. In addition to being marked with all five of the traditional wounds of Christ, she likewise exhibited marks from a crown of thorns and lash marks on her back, and she cried tears of blood. Stranger still, she was known to utter phrases in ancient Aramaic, Hebrew, Greek, and Latin, languages that she did not speak. From 1923 until her death in 1962, Neumann allegedly consumed no food other than the Holy Eucharist and claimed to have drunk no water from 1926 until her death. To test her claims of this mystical fast, on July 1927 a medical doctor and four Franciscan nurses kept a watch on her twenty-four hours a day for two weeks. They confirmed that she had consumed nothing except for one consecrated host a day and had suffered no related effects such as weight loss or dehydration.[185]

CHAPTER 12

Incorruptibles

B ecause we treasure the stories of the lives of the saints and
accordingly seek to emulate their holiness, we want to be
as close to them as possible. We believe with the assurance of
the Catholic Church that they are in heaven with God with the
power and the desire to use their relationship with the Creator
to come to our aid in times of need, just as our friends on earth
would pray for us. We might read the lives of the saints to our
children to give them role models, or consider the saints' spiritual
reflections for inspiration, or pray to saints using prayers found
on their holy cards, or honor their memories with statues in our
home, or celebrate their feast days in special ways. In thanksgiv-
ing to God we might make a pilgrimage to the place where a
saint lived or venerate a saint at a shrine dedicated to him or her.
We might literally walk in a saint's footsteps, as when journey-
ing to St. John Neumann's shrine in Philadelphia, a well-known
location of modern healing miracles, or to the burial place of St.
James in Santiago de Compostela in Spain. According to St. John
Damascene, when we venerate the bodies of saints, it is a form of
praise that we give to God, who raised them to holiness.[186]

This desire for closeness or to be a living part of the communion of holy men and women is taken to an entirely new level
when we look to bring their lives into our own in a tangible way.
Such an attempt at connection with the saints in recognizing the

power and value of relics is an ancient practice that can be found in the Scriptures.

> So Elisha died, and they buried him. Now bands of Moabites used to invade the land in the spring of the year. And as a man was being buried, behold, a marauding band was seen and the man was cast into the grave of Elisha; and as soon as the man touched the bones of Elisha, he revived, and stood on his feet. (2 Kings 13:20–21)

Early Christians also venerated relics, as evidenced by such writings as *The Martyrdom of Polycarp*, written by the Apostolic Fathers in A.D. 150–160.[187] One of the very few eyewitness accounts from the time of the persecutions of Christians, this work mentions veneration of the relics of Polycarp, bishop of Smyrna in the mid-second century.

One of the more unusual and famous relics in Christian history is the liquefying blood of St. Januarius. This bishop and martyr, born in the third century, is the patron saint of Naples, where the faithful gather three times a year at the cathedral to witness the liquefaction of a sample of his blood in a glass vial. On feast days, the relics are taken in procession from the cathedral to the Monastery of Santa Chiara, where the archbishop holds the reliquary up and tilts it to demonstrate that the contents are solid, and then after prayer, the archbishop holds up the vial and tilts it again to demonstrate that liquefaction has taken place. Although the Catholic Church has always supported the participation of the faithful in this feast-day celebration, no official judgment on the phenomenon has been rendered.[188]

Certainly relics were sometimes objects of abuse and commerce during the Middle Ages and the Crusades. Catholics, to the outsider's eye, might be considered to have a strange, superstitious, or even macabre preoccupation with relics, especially if one were to visit the Capuchin church on the Via Veneto in Rome, where the altar and the ceiling are adorned with the remains of monks past. Throughout history the veneration of relics has been questioned from the thinkers of the Enlightenment to the destructive activities of the French Revolution (e.g., the desecration of the corpse of St. Jeanne de Lestonnac in 1640) and the Protestant Reformation (e.g., the burning of the corpse of Bertrand of Garrigue in 1230).[189]

The physical mementos that holy men and women have left behind allow us to connect with them in a primal way. If the saints were verifiably holy while they were alive, so too must the remains of their bodies have some sort of supernatural power effecting canonization, worthy cures, or other miracles or at the very least be tangible reminders of holiness. Many miracles have been attributed to relics, not because of their own power, but because of the holiness of the saints whose relics they are.[190] Because Christians believe in the resurrection of the dead and hope for life everlasting, the veneration of relics has a context.

Relics come in three classes. A first-class relic is from the body of a saint. Typically it is a small bone fragment contained in an ossuary for safekeeping and display. Throughout Europe, relics such as the head and finger of St. Catherine in Siena and the heart and arm of St. Teresa of Ávila in Spain have reminded the faithful of these saints. Other examples of first-class relics include the liquefying blood of St. Januarius and the blood of John Paul II, which was on display in a reliquary for the faithful to see at his beatification in 2012. Second-class relics include a saint's personal effects, those things that the saint touched and interacted with. A swath of fabric from the saint's clothing and a small possession such as a rosary are examples of second-class relics.

A third-class relic is something that has physically touched a first- or second-class relic. In this way the power and remembrance of the saint can go out to a large number of the faithful. Interest in second-class relics can be found even in the New Testament, as Paul's handkerchiefs are thought to be imbued with God's saving power:

> And God did extraordinary miracles by the hands of Paul, so that handkerchiefs or aprons were carried away from his body to the sick, and diseases left them and the evil spirits came out of them. (Acts 19:11–12)

In this spectrum of relics, we have what can be considered one of the most phenomenal spectacles of our Faith: the complete incorruptible bodies of the saints, defying the natural decay found in the laws of nature. No matter how poorly they were buried, in a flimsy coffin or none at all, and in different climates in different parts of the world, miraculously the bodies of several hundred saints remain in a protected state. Many of the incorruptibles look similar to how they did when they died — perhaps with darkened skin due to exposure to the air — with finer details like skin, hair, eyelashes, and fingernails perfectly preserved and muscles still soft and flexible. Typically with this lack of decay, the bodies do not possess the stench of death, and some even are graced with a sweet-smelling fragrance. Some incorruptibles exude fragrant oil or blood years after their burial.

Although the Church clearly spares little effort to put these magnificent bodies of specially graced saints on display, it does not consider incorruptibility to be a guarantee of holiness and no longer gives official recognitions of preservations as it once did through the Congregation of Rites. Prospero Lambertini, in his great work on the canonization of saints, *De Servorum Dei Beatifi-*

catione et de Beatorum Canonizatione, included two chapters *De Cadaverum Incorruptione* in which he outlined the Church's position on incorruptibles, insisting that the cases considered miraculous need be bodies close to perfectly preserved over the course of many years.[191] There are plenty of incorruptibles who have not been canonized, and even more significant, there have been many, many holy men and women who are worthy to be included in the canon of saints but, for whatever reason, were not graced with the special gift of a preserved human body. Unlike other miraculous phenomena such as the stigmata and visions, incorruptibility does not seem to discriminate on the basis of gender, as there is an approximately even split in the numbers of men and women with notably preserved bodies. Likewise it has occurred throughout history to people from all walks of life in many countries of the world.

Throughout the world and its many cultures, preserved corpses exist due to three distinct possibilities: deliberate preservation, accidental preservation, and incorruptibility.[192] There are some incorruptibles outside the Catholic Church, if you consider the deliberately preserved mummies of Egypt, Peru (Incans), Babylon, and Tibet as well as others, such as Lenin, who have gone through an extensive preservation process. Other corpses that are at rest in the perfect atmospheric conditions may be accidentally protected.[193] Typically no matter how good the embalming process, they do not appear as well preserved — often dried out, brittle, and discolored — as the flexible body of a saint spared the ravages of time by God without the need for an advanced preservation process or ideal temperatures.

According to Joan Carroll Cruz in her definitive book on the topic, *The Incorruptibles: A Study of the Incorruption of the Bodies of Various Catholic Saints and Beati,* "the incorruptibles, for the most part, were never embalmed or treated in any manner."[194] In fact, many corpses remain magnificently intact despite the various attempts to check the body, redress it with fresh vestments, or translate it to new burial locations. Oftentimes, due to poverty, conditions, and poor burial materials and practices, bodies are not protected from excessive moisture or other factors that would hasten the decomposition process. Despite all that, Christian history is filled with stories of incorruptible saints.

First seen in the body of the early Roman martyr St. Cecilia in the second century,[195] incorruption is a gift generally exclusively claimed by Catholics, partly because it is an element of the tradition of the Church to venerate (and obtain) relics but also to inspect the corpses prior to such proceedings as beatifications, canonizations, and translations between burial locations. Other than the Orthodox churches, most other religions do not have these practices. There is an overwhelming sense of respect and at times fascination with the body of a holy person in Catholic tradition. The body of Catherine of Bologna (1413–1463), the patron saint of artists, was found to be in perfect condition, emitting sweet fragrances, and considered to have wrought many miracles. So many visitors wished to see the body that for twelve years her fellow sisters brought out the body on a stretcher before later devising a seated display for her body in the chapel.

Despite the awe-inspiring and scientifically inexplicable reality of this strange phenomenon, the simple fact is that there is more to understanding incorruptibility than first meets the eye. Not all incorruptibles are preserved to the same level of completeness, nor are they preserved for the same amount of time. There have been bodies whose coffins have been opened for hundreds of years for beatification and canonization or translations between various churches and burial locations or routine incorruptibility checks. Their bodies may have been preserved rather perfectly for a long period — hundreds of years even —

and then, for some unknown reason, begin to degrade in appearance. Other bodies, incorrupt for hundreds of years, suddenly succumb to the conditions and decay. From some of the bodies that have dried and turned brown, hearts and other organs have successfully been removed.

Some of the incorruptible bodies that look perfect in photographs — including those of St. Bernadette Soubirous of Lourdes fame and St. Padre Pio — in fact do have at least a light wax masking (and in some, embalming fluid) to make their appearance more presentable.[196] A skeptic might ask, "If God wants to preserve a body perfectly and he has the power to do so, why not keep the bodies perfect for all time?" Even the slightest bit of imperfection — browning, wrinkling, or shrinking — on a supposedly preserved corpse seems strange in the face of that line of questioning. For whatever reason, God provides us with this mystery and allows the effects of nature not to be completely suspended indefinitely. What is the purpose of incorruptibility? Perhaps it is an opportunity to bolster our faith and to remind us simultaneously of our mortality and of eternal realities that await us.

The bodies of some saints remain perfectly flexible after many years. St. Francis Xavier (1506–1552), missionary to the Far East and cofounder of the Society of Jesus, remained in a state of perfect preservation for 142 years despite a series of translations and amputations. The body of Spanish mystic and poet St. John of the Cross (1542–1591) remains flexible to this very day.[197] In some rare instances, only a part of the body is perfectly preserved. In the case of St. Anthony of Padua, a Franciscan friar from Portugal known for his preaching, his body composed normally to dust and bones, but the remains of his tongue, larynx, and jaw are well preserved in the Basilica of St. Anthony in Padua as a testament to his preaching.[198]

Unfortunately, in some cases, the bodies of holy men and women, such as Bl. Peter Ghigenzi,[199] reported to be perfectly preserved, have been lost due to fires and other disasters, either accidental or purposeful attacks by enemies of the Church. Other saints were dismembered before or after their burial, and their extracted parts continue to be preserved. The removed arms of St. Nicholas of Tolentino are still incorrupt.[200] St. Andrew Bobola (1591–1657), the Polish Jesuit missionary, after hours of torture and mutilation, was killed by the sword. His body was later discovered among many other decayed corpses, still bloody and in a state of perfect preservation, which was recognized officially by the Congregation of Rites in 1835.[201]

Other saints' corpses were perfectly incorruptible for centuries and now have become dark and stiff. St. Isidore the Farmer remained in good condition for more than eight hundred years before succumbing to the natural processes of decomposition.[202] Other saints' bodies have changed even more dramatically from their initial state of perfection. In the case of St. Charbel Makhlouf (1828–1898), a monk from Lebanon renowned for miracles, his grave had been opened several times, and each time "it has been noticed that his bleeding body still has its flexibility as if it were alive."[203] Fr. Joseph Mahfouz, the postulator of the cause, certified that in 1965 the body of St. Charbel was still preserved intact with no alteration. In 1976 he again witnessed the opening of the grave and discovered that the body was completely decomposed with only the skeleton remaining.

An extremely common accompanying phenomenon seems to be the discovery of liquid oozing from the body. Oil flows continuously from the body of Bl. Matthia Nazzarei of Matelica, who died in 1320. In the case of St. Charbel, a bright light was reported surrounding his tomb years after his death. The superiors opened it to find his body still intact and oozing a bloody substance.[204] St. Agnes of Montepulciano's body also exuded fragrant oil after death.[205] The body of Ven. Mother Mariana de Jesus, the seventeenth-century Spanish nun who received visions of Our Lady of Good Success in Quito, Ecuador, sweats fragrant oil to this day.[206] Other saints have exuded fresh blood many years after they died. Forty years after his death, the arms of St. Nicholas of Tolentino were ripped off his body by a relic-gathering lay brother who, to his surprise, left bloody evidence of his theft everywhere. Pope Benedict XIV noted the occurrence as miraculous.[207]

The companion phenomenon to the exuding of oils is the "odor of sanctity" or the fragrant smell accompanying the body of a saintly person. This has been detected on many saints at the moment of their deaths, but in some cases the fragrance persists for many years. Observers noted the smell at the grave of St. Albert the Great 200 years after his death and at the grave of Bl. Angelo of Borgo San Sepolcro 276 years after his death.[208]

There are many accounts of miracles attributed to the incorrupt bodies of saints, and a few are so spectacular that they seem to be the stuff of legends. In a couple of cases, the postmortem animation of a corpse was reported. When St. Catherine of Siena arrived to venerate the body of St. Agnes of Montepulciano, Agnes's body stirred.[209] Bl. Antonio Vici's body is credited with exorcizing a girl afflicted by demons who viewed the preserved corpse.[210] Other phenomenal reports involve mysterious illuminations. Accounts of St. Guthlac, St. Louis Bertrand, St. John of the Cross, and St. Charbel tell of a bright light accompanying their incorrupt bodies.[211]

With advances in modern embalming, including the use of formaldehyde and other chemicals used to stave off natural decomposition, short of the discovery of new incorruptibles, the bodies of saints experiencing this miraculous preservation may be a phenomenon of the past, as it will become impossible to rule out chemical intervention. Visitors to St. Peter's in Rome have surely seen the perfectly preserved body of St. John XXIII, which ostensibly owes its perfection at least (or mostly) to a specialized embalming process and the airtight coffin in which he is laid.[212]

Science has not been able to identify the cause of incorruptibility, short of pointing to favorable atmospheric conditions that have been shown to preserve to a degree some bodies of non-sainted persons in rare cases. It is thought that for natural mummification to occur, the bodies would need to undergo a swift burial process in an ideally dry environment. The burial of several incorruptibles was postponed so that the faithful could venerate their bodies — for example, St. Bernardine of Siena and St. Angela Merici each lay in state for almost thirty days — which would disqualify them as being subject to the ideal initial conditions of the process.[213]

The frail and rigid characteristics of these "accidentally" preserved bodies and the very imperfect conditions surrounding many of the well-preserved saintly incorruptibles renders the scientific answer mute. Moisture is the key agent in the dissolution of a buried body, and numerous saints were discovered with this detrimental factor affecting at least their garments — such as St. Catherine of Genoa and St. Madeliene Sophie Barat[214] — and in some cases even their enclosure. The coffins of St. Charles Borromeo, St. Teresa of Ávila, and St. Catherine Labouré were all severely damaged by moisture, but the saints inside were discovered to be in perfect condition.[215] Some saints, including St. Catherine of Bologna, St. Pacifico of San Severino, and St. Charbel Makhlouf, were buried without the benefit of a coffin and were preserved in a remarkable state of perfection.

Skeptics point to the variability in the quality of the corpses and the baffling fact that commonly the bodies are soft, flexible, and otherwise perfectly preserved for many years, even centuries, and then succumb to nature and exhibit some or total decay. After a body is discovered to be in this miraculous state, extra effort is often put into preserving them in protective chambers, fresh clothing, and occasionally even embalming fluid.[216] Such later interventions might raise eyebrows and doubts for some about the claimed lack of previous preservation attempts and deceptions. The simple fact remains that in many cases throughout history, the bodies of holy men and women were unearthed many years after their deaths and survived sometimes for centuries in perfect condition, inexplicably giving people a nearly exact glimpse of what they looked like in life.

CHAPTER 13

Stigmata

W hen walking around the streets of Rome, one might notice the styles of habits that are worn by the various orders of priests and nuns stationed in the Eternal City. One of the
most striking is that of the Brigittine Order, founded by visionary
mystic St. Birgitta of Sweden, which features a distinctive metal
headdress, the "Crown of the Five Holy Wounds." It has five red
stones to remember the Five Wounds of Christ on the Cross. The
wounds of Christ are widely depicted in medieval art, such as in
Caravaggio's *Incredulity of Saint Thomas* (1602). The writings of
saints such as Alphonsus Ligouri (1696–1787) and the devotions
and devotionals of the Passionists, such as the Five Wound Beads
and the Chaplet of the Five Wounds introduced by Ven. Sister
Mary Martha Chambon, have brought the sufferings of Christ
into focus.

Beyond such symbolic clothing and other physical and intel-
lectual aids to profound meditation on Christ's sufferings, numerous saints and others throughout history have physically born
the wounds of Christ on their bodies. St. Paul, in his letter to
the Galatians, alludes to the power associated with being even
just symbolically connected to Christ in this way: "Henceforth
let no man trouble me; for I bear on my body the marks of Jesus" (6:17). Most of these mystics have united themselves with
the profound suffering of Christ on a deep spiritual level. They

manifest on their bodies nonsuperficial wounds that correspond to those suffered by Christ during his Crucifixion. The presence of these wounds — or stigmata, "marks" — is often (mistakenly) taken to be a divine sign of holiness conferred on a living person. The Church, however, does not take them into account during the canonization process or elsewhere as a guarantee of a person's life of virtue. Such cases have a potential for great scandal and embarrassment. In investigating a case of stigmata, the Church is watchful of the humility of the person suffering the wounds and examines whether the wounds are superficial and respond to medical treatment.

Authentic wounds are extremely painful and typically are not accompanied by a foul odor.[217] True stigmata, although manifested by an individual, are meant for the Church at large as a reminder of the profound sacrifice of Christ. If it were not for the accompanying suffering, the wounds would be meaningless, merely for show, and be a dangerous temptation to pride. In addition to the pain, many stigmatics also experience great spiritual ecstasy. They are allegedly often given many spiritual gifts in addition to receiving the wounds of Christ. It is said that it is not uncommon for them to experience visions, levitation, and healing powers. Perhaps most commonly associated with stigmata is inedia. One of history's most famous stigmatics, Bl. Anne Catherine Emmerich, a frail and sickly German nun, was confined to bed where she received the stigmata and reported visions of the Blessed Virgin Mary along with vivid spiritual insights on the life and Passion of Jesus Christ. The most well-known modern stigmatic, St. Padre Pio of Pietrelcina (1887–1968), was surrounded by a panoply of alleged mystical gifts, including visions, bilocation, and the ability to read souls. Servant of God Maria Esperanza de Bianchini (1928–2004) allegedly exhibited all these powers and more, including claiming to receive a vision of Padre Pio himself, who provided her with spiritual direction and his mantle.[218]

Tradition seems to indicate that the very first true stigmatic in recorded history was St. Francis of Assisi (1182–1286). Art throughout the ages, including Giotto's *St. Francis Receiving the Stigmata* (c. 1295–1300), has depicted the great patron saint of Italy and founder of the Franciscans in this ecstatic moment being marked with the wounds of Christ.[219] This event is said to have occurred on September 14, 1224, the feast of the Exaltation of the Cross. Brother Leo, who had been with Francis at the time, provided the first clear account of the phenomenon of stigmata: "Suddenly he saw a vision of a seraph, a six-winged angel on a cross. This angel gave him the gift of the five wounds of Christ." In his classic analysis of miracles, *The Physical Phenomena of Mysticism*, Rev. Herbert Thurston skeptically notes that Francis's case is the first, after which, "throughout the world, other unquestionable cases of stigmata began to occur even among people who were much lower than Francis in religious stature, and have continued to occur without intermission ever since."[220]

The Italian friar was the first of about 404 stigmatics in recorded history.[221] The first priest to exhibit the wounds was twentieth-century mystic St. Padre Pio of Pietrelcina, whose scientifically well-documented marks persisted for about fifty years until they healed at his death. Most stigmatics follow a consistent profile, as they are not only Catholics but typically (as many as 66 percent[222]) have entered religious life. Historically they have come from traditionally Catholic countries with the vast majority of cases being reported from Italy (more than a third) and most of the others stemming from Spain, France, and Portugal.[223] In the twentieth century, a wider variety of countries have seen claims, and a handful of Anglicans have reported the phenomena as well.[224]

Throughout history, most stigmatics — some put the number as high as 80 percent[225] — have been women. In the last hundred years the distribution is more balanced, with 55 percent women. No viable scientific explanation has been produced for this trend that corresponds to the fact that the majority of visionaries are also women. Just considering the revelations related to the Sacred Heart devotion alone, St. Margaret Mary Alacoque, St. Mecthilde, and St. Gertrude have been the primary recipients of this message.[226] Teresa of Ávila, the great saint and Doctor of the Church, had remarked that the Holy Spirit generally selects women for these supernatural graces.[227]

A key aspect of the stigmata that has been attacked by skeptics is that not all cases are the same, with somewhat varying formations, locations, and depths of the wounds, depending on the recipient. The most common locations of the wounds are the five Crucifixion wound locations honored by Christian tradition and the Brigittine habit, for example: nail marks in both hands and in both feet and a pierced side from what is traditionally known as the Holy Lance of Longinus. Others receive wounds on their foreheads corresponding to the crown of thorns, and still others show marks on their backs from scourging or cry tears of blood. Some saints have received the full set of five wounds, and others have received partial stigmata.

St. Rita of Cascia (1381–1457), the patron saint of impossible causes, was a nun known for her meditations on the Passion of Christ. When she prayed that she might participate in the suffering of Christ and alleviate some of his pain, she received a thorn wound in her forehead that is often included in her iconography. Hers is the one known exception to the odor of sanctity that usually accompanies stigmata, and she spent fifteen years in seclusion due to the hideous odor that came from her stigmata. Later, three days before her death and during her burial, her wounds began to emit a sweet odor.

On March 10, 1918 (the same year Padre Pio received his stigmata), German mystic Therese Neumann received the five wounds of Christ in the style of hardened flesh forming nails, as St. Francis had, and then years later bore nine crown-of-thorns marks and marks of scourging on her back. In all, her body was marked with at least forty-five distinct wounds.[228] Her condition was well documented with photos by scientists. In a few very rare cases, such as in the modern cases of Fr. Zlatko Sudac of Croatia since 1999 and Myrna Nazzour of Damascus since 1983, bleeding has occurred in the shape of a cross on the recipients' foreheads.

A few saints have claimed invisible stigmata, whereby in humility they suffer the pain of wounds that cannot be seen. St. Teresa of Ávila wrote in her *Autobiography* about a mystical wound in her heart, known as transverberation; this was later confirmed by doctors who in 1872 posthumously verified that she had a perforation in her heart, which is now kept in a reliquary in Alba de Tormes. St. Catherine of Siena, an influential Italian nun, a Doctor of the Church, and one of history's greatest mystics, received the five wounds of the stigmata in Pisa in 1375 as she weighed in on the formation of alliances and the proposal to start a new Crusade. According to Raymond of Capua's biography, she received the stigmata, but at her request it remained invisible to everyone but her.[229] St. Gemma Galgani (1878–1903) and St. Catherine de' Ricci, a Florentine Dominican of the sixteenth century, had similar requests that were honored. Bl. Marie of the Incarnation, O.C.D., called the "Mother of Carmel in France" and known for her charity to the poor and the sick, also claimed these unseen wounds of Christ along with other mystical gifts, such as healing, prophecy and the ability to read souls.

Often at the death of a saint with invisible stigmata, the wounds manifest openly as an authenticating sign of God for all to see. At the death of St. Catherine of Siena, the stigmata appeared visibly and were noted by Popes Urban VII and Benedict XIV.[230]

Some saints reported invisible stigmata before they received the visible manifestation. St. Padre Pio noted this suffering as many as eight years before his wounds appeared. In writing to his spiritual director, he claimed that "his whole body was burning in an indescribable manner,"[231] and later that he felt "on fire" and suffered "acute pain" and "spiritual languor."[232] St. John of the Cross explained the phenomenon moving from spiritual to physical in the case of St. Francis:

> If God sometime permits an effect to extend to the bodily senses in the fashion in which it existed interiorly, the wound and sore appears outwardly, as happened when the seraphim wounded St. Francis.[233]

While he suffered for some years with the invisible variety, Padre Pio's stigmata was first visibly manifested on September 20, 1918, when he was in prayer before the crucifix in the choir loft. Great pain accompanied the five wounds with which he was stricken. He typically wore fingerless gloves to hide the wounds from the public eye but subjected himself to many investigations over the years, including those initiated by his local bishop and the Holy See, who had become doubtful about the authenticity of the condition. Physicians found nothing out of the ordinary in his skeletal structure and noted the smoothness of the wounds and the lack of edema that would have been expected.[234] Skeptics have doubted the natural origin of the wounds and suspected that he used carbolic acid obtained from a local pharmacy for the sterilization of needles used on the boys to fight the Spanish Flu. The accusations were dismissed during the thorough investigations during Padre Pio's beatification process.[235]

Even among the most famous and reputable stigmatics, there has been a great variability in the wounds. Photographs show that the wounds pierced Padre Pio's palms through to the back of his hands, whereas St. Francis reportedly had his stigmata through his wrists. St. Francis's first biographer, Thomas of Celano, describes the wounds in *First Life of St. Francis* (1230):

> His wrists and feet seemed to be pierced by nails, with the heads of the nails appearing on his wrists and on the upper sides of his feet, the points appearing on the other side. The marks were round on the palm of each hand but elongated on the other side, and small pieces of flesh jutting out from the rest took on the appearance of the nail-ends, bent and driven back. In the same way the marks of nails were impressed on his feet and projected beyond the rest of the flesh. Moreover, his right side had a large wound as if it had been pierced with a spear, and it often bled so that his tunic and trousers were soaked with his sacred blood.[236]

Such a variance might indicate the possibility that the wounds are generated in the locations that the recipient, in meditation, associates with Christ's suffering. Skeptics have pointed to a correspondence between artwork and crucifixes owned by the stigmatic and the marks on their bodies.[237] Other anatomists suggest it is impossible to crucify someone suspended by the palms, thus prompting skeptics to suggest that the authentic wounds would correspond to the wrists and all palm-marked stigmatics should be disregarded as frauds.[238]

The duration and timing of the wounds can differ among stigmatics as well. Some might exhibit the wounds for a specific time with some meaning — for example, only on Fridays at 3 p.m.

or during Lent. Therese Neuman received her last set of wounds on Good Friday in 1929, and Myrna Nazzour had wounds open and close on her head, hands, feet, and side on Holy Thursday every third year, when the Eastern and Western churches celebrate Easter on the same day. Some have taken this to be a reflection of the wish of Jesus in the Gospel of John for Christian unity: "ut unum sint" ("that they may be one"; Jn 17:11).

Some have experienced the stigmata on a less predictable basis, and others have suffered the wounds continuously. The stigmata of St. Francis was continuous but only for two years, until his death on October 3, 1226. Those of Therese Neumann lasted forty-eight years and those of St. Pio fifty years.

There have certainly been cases of false stigmata of several varieties. While St. Francis is recognized as the first authentic stigmatic, there were others before him, including a fraudulent man from Oxford who in 1222 not only claimed to bear the five wounds of Christ but to be Christ himself.[239] In his *Stigmata: A Medieval Phenomenon in a Modern Age*, author Ted Harrison asserts that stigmata can occur as a result of many factors with no common thread in how it originates in all stigmatics.[240] Skeptics who insist that the marks are a psychosomatic manifestation of suffering generated by the recipient might point to the fact that there are no recorded cases prior to the thirteenth century, when art began to focus on the humanity of Christ.[241] Theoretically, a person might be overwhelmed with the sufferings of Christ and penetrated by a great love, resulting in a physical reproduction of the wounds of Christ. Although it is admirable to offer up such suffering, such a person would not be participating in a supernatural event.

Some people have suggested that the phenomenon is the result of such psychological effects, but even according to professional skeptic Joe Nickell, author of *Looking for a Miracle*, there have been no successful reproductions of a stigmata-like effect using the power of suggestion in hypnosis. According to Rev. Charles M. Carty in *The Stigmata and Modern Science*, a well-regarded atheist physician from Paris, Jean-Martin Charcot (1825–1893), known as the founder of modern neurology, conducted many tests on patients considered hysterical in unsuccessful attempts to produce stigmata-like marks on the body. Dr. Joseph Jules Déjérine, who succeeded him, acknowledged that at his clinic there was never a single fully successful case of generating bleeding wounds among the large number of psychopathic patients experimented on.[242] With this being the modern consensus, the hypothesis that stigmata are the result of hysteria can be safely ruled out.

Carty also addresses the possibility of diabolically produced stigmata and suggests it is a nonexistent modern phenomenon. He quotes Cardinal Giovanni Bona (1609–1674), who suggests that the devil has successfully executed such trickery: "The marks of the wounds of Christ can be imitated and impressed by the fiend, as so many examples too painfully have proven."[243] Michael Freze, author of *They Bore the Wounds of Christ*, suggests that the devil has produced the marks of the stigmata "many times in the course of Christian history."[244] There have been no known modern cases of such deception — which, of course, requires the participation and free consent of the recipient — but one should not forget the extreme case of Sr. Magdalena de la Cruz in sixteenth-century Cordoba, Spain. The story is told of a girl who had an encounter with the devil, later became abbess of a Franciscan convent, and gained a great reputation for sanctity, including among Spanish nobility and Queen Isabella. For thirty-nine years she exhibited many mystical gifts but was subject to punishment from the Inquisition[245] when she later confessed on her deathbed that her powers had been obtained through a pact with the devil. The stigmata and her other gifts disappeared when she repented of her sins.[246]

Throughout history, many people have exhibited stigmata-like marks that occurred naturally, or were part of a deliberately perpetrated hoax, or were self-inflicted wounds due to self-mutilation or psychological disorders.[247] Freze acknowledges:

> There have been cases where some overly fanatic souls have so desired the Sacred Stigmata that they have intentionally wounded themselves with knives, picks, etc., in order to produce false impressions to others that they were extraordinary saints.[248]

According to skeptical author Ted Harrison in his *Stigmata: A Medieval Phenomenon in a Modern Age*, not all marks of natural origin need be considered hoaxes. Some alleged stigmatics might have marked themselves to suffer with Christ as a form of piety. Perhaps they had no intent of making a public display of their pious attempt at participation in the Crucifixion.[249]

Although there certainly have been those whose claims of stigmata are questionable, the *Catholic Dictionary* tells us that the "Church considers the three hundred recorded manifestations of the stigmata as signs of particular favor by the Lord," who allows certain individuals to participate physically in the suffering of the Crucifixion. This participation is considered a distinct privilege granted by the Lord to those who are exceptionally holy individuals.

CONCLUSION

M iracles provide a somewhat universal answer to that profound and authentic hunger for what is good and true, and they serve as reminders not only that God is with us but that he is truly involved in the spiritual and physical well-being and protection of all of us as his children. His glory is made manifest in the miracles he provides.

We are all familiar with the biblical accounts of miracles that display the majesty and power of God demonstrated for us in the person of Jesus Christ.[250] Those accounts need not be relegated to a past age. Miracles throughout Christian history in the lives of the saints (and those of us still striving to be saints) are awe-inspiring events that excite us and lead us closer to Christ and his Church. Yet these matters do have the potential for distraction and uncertainty, so we should find comforting reassurance in knowing that the Church takes such pastoral care to protect us from claims that are unworthy of belief and those elements that could endanger our souls. It is important to remember that no matter how great or weak our faith is in modern-day miracles (even the fully approved and celebrated devotions of the Church), it truly doesn't matter — we are guided to Christ, who is the center of our lives and the true object of our faith.

These experiences of the supernatural throughout history serve as shining examples of God's great providence and bring to light the truths of our eternal destiny. We owe the Creator everything for willing us into existence and sustaining our every living moment. As an omnipotent and omniscient being, he needs nothing from us. All that we can offer is the unabashed love of a child for his Father and the gift of our faith as we hope to be joined with him for eternity.

NOTES

1 Preface to *Heroic Virtue: A Portion of the Treatise of Benedict XIV on the Beatification and Canonization of the Servants of God*, vol. 1 (translated from the original five-volume work in Latin, *De Servorum Dei Beatificatione et de Beatorum Canonizatione*) (New York: Edward Dunigan and Brothers, 1850), xii–xiii.

2 Dwight Longenecker, "On Miracles, Magicians, and Manichees," in *The Quest for the Creed* (Chestnut Ridge, NY: Crossroad, 2013), at *Catholic Exchange*, August 7, 2014, retrieved August 3, 2015, http://catholicexchange.com/miracles-magicians-manichees.

3 Gary R. Habermas and Antony G.N. Flew, *Did Jesus Rise from the Dead?: The Resurrection Debate* (San Francisco: Harper and Row, 1987), 7. Flew later became a deist.

4 "O my Jesus, forgive us our sins, save us from the fires of hell. Lead all souls to heaven, especially those most in need of thy mercy." World Apostolate of Fatima, http://wafusa.org/the-apostolate/prayers/.

5 "A Christogram is a monogram or combination of letters that forms an abbreviation for the name of Jesus Christ, traditionally used as a Christian symbol." "Christogram," *Wikipedia*, last modified November 25, 2014, accessed August 3, 2015, https://en.wikipedia.org/wiki/Christogram.

6 *Lumen Gentium* (Dogmatic Constitution on the Church), no. 5.

7 Joseph Cardinal Ratzinger, *The Message of Fatima*, accessed August 3, 2015, http://www.vatican.va/roman_curia/congregations/cfaith/documents/rc_con_cfaith_doc_20000626_message-Fatima_en.html.

8 Joseph Cardinal Ratzinger, post-synodal apostolic exhortation *Verbum Domini*, no. 14, accessed August 3, 2015, http://www.vatican.va/holy_father/benedict_xvi/apost_exhortations/documents/hf_ben-xvi_exh_20100930_verbum-domini_en.html.

⁹ See Ralph M. McInerny, *Miracles: A Catholic View* (Huntington, IN: Our Sunday Visitor, 1986), 121.

¹⁰ Vatican I, Session 3: Dogmatic Constitution on the Catholic Faith, canon 4.3; posted at EWTN, accessed August 3, 2015, https://www.ewtn.com/library/COUNCILS/V1.HTM.

¹¹ Dietrich von Hildebrand, *Trojan Horse in the City of God* (Manchester, NH: Sophia Institute Press, 1999), 51.

¹² "Miraculous Apparition in the Sky Made Georgians Run during Military Actions in South Ossetia," Interfax, July 1, 2009, retrieved July 31, 2015, http://www.interfax-religion .com/?act=news&div=6177.

¹³ Michael Ott, "Our Lady of the Snow," *Catholic Encyclopedia*, vol. 11 (New York: Robert Appleton Company, 1911), retrieved August 3, 2015, http://www.newadvent.org/cathen/11361c.htm.

¹⁴ *Calendarium Romanum* (Libreria Editrice Vaticana, 1969), 133.

¹⁵ *Conciliorum*, 775.31–35; quoted in McInerny, *Miracles*, 124.

¹⁶ Joan Carroll Cruz, *Eucharistic Miracles: And the Eucharistic Phenomena in the Lives of the Saints* (Charlotte, NC: TAN Books, 2010), 226.

¹⁷ Joseph Cardinal Ratzinger with Vittorio Messori, *The Ratzinger Report* (San Francisco: Ignatius Press, 1986), 111.

¹⁸ Ratzinger, *The Message of Fatima*.

¹⁹ "Norms and Process for Judging Private Revelation," University of Dayton International Marian Research Institute, "Mary Page," accessed August 3, 2015, http://campus.udayton.edu/mary /resources/newsltr.html.

²⁰ Fr. Peter Joseph, "Apparitions True and False," *Inside the Vatican* (March 2005): 32–39.

²¹ Autobiography of St. Margaret Mary Alacoque.

²² Ibid.

²³ Joan Carroll Cruz, *The Incorruptibles: A Study of the Incorruption of the Bodies of Various Catholic Saints and Beati* (Rockford, IL: TAN Books and Publishers, 1977), 36.

²⁴ Interview with Denis Searby, professor at Stockholm University, chairman of classics, who is the translator of *The Revelations of St. Birgitta of Sweden*, Miracle Hunter, Radio Maria, August 12, 2014.

25 See Fr. Edward D. O'Connor, *Marian Apparitions Today* (Santa Barbara: Queenship Publishing, 1996), 122–123; Marjorie Reeves, *Prophecy in the Later Middle Ages: A Study of Joachimism* (Oxford: Clarendon Press, 1969), 441.

26 Council of Trent, session 25, "On the Invocation, Veneration, and Relics of Saints and on Sacred Images," accessed August 3, 2015, http://history.hanover.edu/texts/trent/trentall.html.

27 Cruz, *Eucharistic Miracles*, 95–99.

28 *L'Osservatore Romano*, June 15, 1966, 1. *L'Osservatore Romano* appears in the late afternoon, bearing the date of the following day.

29 René Laurentin, "East and West: Convergences and Differences on the Virgin Mary," paper presented at the Twelfth International Mariological Congress, Czestochowa, Poland, August 18–23, 1996.

30 Sacred Congregation for the Doctrine of the Faith, introduction to the *Norms Regarding the Manner of Proceeding in the Discernment of Presumed Apparitions or Revelations*, Vatican website, May 24, 2012, accessed August 3, 2015, http://www.vatican.va/roman_curia/congregations/cfaith/documents/rc_con_cfaith_doc_19780225_norme-apparizioni_en.html.

31 *Etoile Notre Dame*, October 2006.

32 Kevin Symonds, "Our Lady of All Nations: Approved?" Catholic Lane, August 6, 2012, accessed August 3, 2015, http://catholiclane.com/olan-approved/. Msgr. Charles J. Scicluna, Orientamenti dottrinali e competenze del vescovo diocesano e della Congregazione per la Dottrina della Fede nel discernimento delle apparizioni mariane in "Pontificia Academia Mariana Internationalis," Apparitiones Beatae Mariae Virginis in Historia, Fide, Teologia. Acta Congressus marioligici–mariani internationalis in Civitate Lourdes Anno 2008 celebrati. Studia in sessionibus plenaria exhibita, vol 1, PAMI, Città del Vaticano 2010, 329–356.

33 Most Reverend David Laurin Ricken, D.D., J.C.L., *Decree on the Authenticity of the Apparitions of 1859 at the Shrine of Our Lady of Good Help Diocese of Green Bay*, Archdiocese of Green Bay website, accessed August 3, 2015, http://www.gbdioc.org/images/stories

/Evangelization_Worship/Shrine/Documents/Shrine-of-Our-
Lady-of-Good-Help.pdf.
34 International Marian Research Institute, "Norms and Process for
Judging Private Revelations," University of Dayton "Mary Page,"
retrieved August 1, 2015, http://campus.udayton.edu/mary//
resources/newsltr.html.
35 Notification by Sacred Congregation regarding alleged
apparitions, *L'Osservatore Romano*, June 27, 1974, 2.
36 "Documents of the Congregation for the Doctrine of the Faith,"
published in 2006 (Document 22, p. 90).
37 Stefano M. Paci, "The Tears of Akita," *30 Days*, July–August 1990,
45.
38 International Marian Research Institute, "Apparitions in the
News," University of Dayton's "Mary Page," accessed August 3,
2105, campus.udayton.edu/mary/respub/apprdoc.html.
39 "Unapproved Apparitions," The Miracle Hunter, accessed May 1,
2012, http://www.miraclehunter.com/marian_apparitions
/unapproved_apparitions.
40 Sarah Delaney, "Claims of Apparitions of Mary Met with
Skepticism, Book Shows," Catholic News Service, December 13,
2010, accessed August 3, 2015, http://www.catholicnews.com
/services/englishnews/2010/claims-of-apparitions-of-mary-met-
with-skepticism-book-shows.cfm.
41 "Bishop Approved Apparitions," The Miracle Hunter, accessed
August 3, 2105, http://miraclehunter.com/marian_apparitions
/approved_apparitions/bishop.html.
42 Janice T. Connell, *The Spiritual Journey of George Washington*
(CreateSpace, 2013), 134.
43 Cause Opened by Monterey Diocese," Catholic News
Agency, March 18, 2012, accessed August 3, 2015, http://www
.catholicnewsagency.com/news/california-womans-sainthood-
cause-opened-by-monterey-diocese/.
44 Glenn Dallaire, "The Miraculous Story of Claude Newman and
His Conversion through the Intercession of the Virgin Mary,"
Mystics of the Church, accessed August 3, 2015, http://www

.mysticsofthechurch.com/2011/12/miraculous-story-of-claude-newman-his.html.

[45] Sandra Zimdars-Swartz, "Religious Experience and Public Cult: The Case of Mary Ann Van Hoof," *Journal of Religion and Health* 28 (1989): 36–57.

[46] "History of the Bayside Apparitions" Apparitions of the Virgin Mary to Veronica Leuken website, accessed May 1, 2012, http://www.rosesfromheaven.com/bayside_history.htm.

[47] Synod of Bishops, Special Assembly for America: *Encounter with the Living Jesus Christ: The Way to Conversion, Communion and Solidarity in America*, August 8, 1996, 33.

[48] Quoted in Matt C. Abbot, "The U.S. Marian Apparition Burnout," Renew America, July 21, 2007, accessed August 3, 2015, http://www.renewamerica.com/columns/abbott/070721.

[49] For the original text, see *Acta Apostolicae Sedis* 88, no. 12 (December 5, 1996): 956–957. The citation here is from a clarification of the original notification on Vassula Ryden that the CDF released to the press: *L'Osservatore Romano*, December 4, 1996, 12, posted at EWTN, accessed August 3, 2015, http://www.ewtn.com/library/CURIA/CDFRYDN2.HTM.

[50] "Joseph Januszkiewicz, Malboro, New Jersey, U.S.A. 1989–1994 (The Yellow Rose of Peace)," accessed Sept. 29, 2015, http://catholicrevelations.org/PR/joe%20januszkiewitz.htm.

[51] Peter Heintz, *A Guide to Apparitions of Our Blessed Virgin Mary* (Sacramento: Gabriel Press, 1995), 632–633.

[52] Kristy Nabhan-Warren, *The Virgin of El Barrio: Marian Apparitions, Catholic Evangelizing, and Mexican American Activism* (New York: New York University Press, 2005), 224.

[53] Heintz, *A Guide to Apparitions of Our Blessed Virgin Mary*, 666–667.

[54] Conyers — Our Loving Mother, official website of Nancy Fowler, accessed August 3, 2015, http://www.ourlovingmother.org/.

[55] Heintz, *A Guide to Apparitions of Our Blessed Virgin Mary*, 653–663.

[56] "About John Leary" John Leary website, accessed May 1, 2012, http://www.johnleary.com/index.php/about/.

[57] Heintz, *A Guide to Apparitions of Our Blessed Virgin Mary*, 636–638.

58 "About the Visionary," Holy Love Ministry, accessed May 1, 2012, http://www.holylove.org/about_visionary.php.

59 "Anne, a Lay Apostle: Anne's Introduction" Direction for Our Times, accessed August 3, 2015, http://directionforourtimes.com /anne-a-lay-apostle/.

60 "Unapproved Apparition Claims," The Miracle Hunter, accessed May 1, 2012, http://www.miraclehunter.com/marian_ apparitions/unapproved_apparitions.

61 Donal Foley. "False visions which followed Lourdes" *Theotokos Catholic Books*, accessed September 29, 2015, http://www .theotokos.org.uk/pages/unapprov/falseapp/flourdes.html.

62 "Prayer Gatherings," Caritas of Birmingham, accessed May 1, 2012, http://www.caritasofbirmingham.com/caritas-prayer-gatherings.html.

63 Medjugorje Visionaries," Medjugorje.com, accessed August 3, 2015, http://www.medjugorje.com/medjugorje/medjugorje-visionaries/581-ivan.html.

64 Pat Archbold, "Medjugorje Bombshell," *National Catholic Register*, November 6, 2013, accessed August 3, 2015, http://www .ncregister.com/blog/pat-archbold/medjugorje-bombshell.

65 Patricia Treece, *Nothing Short of a Miracle* (Manchester, NH: Sophia Institute Press, 2013), xxix.

66 Ibid.

67 "Lourdes: 69th Official Miracle Announced," Independent Catholic News, July 19, 2013, accessed August 3, 2015, http:// www.indcatholicnews.com/news.php?viewStory=22985.

68 Randy Sullivan, *The Miracle Detective: An Investigation of Holy Visions* (New York: Atlantic Monthly Press, 2004), cited in "No Miracles Allowed: Historical/Critical Exegesis," *Metaphysical Catholic* (blog), June 16, 2011, accessed August 3, 2015, http:// metaphysicalcatholic.blogspot.com/2011/06/no-miracles-required-historicalcritical.html.

69 Camillo Beccari, "Beatification and Canonization," *Catholic Encyclopedia*, vol. 2 (New York: Robert Appleton Company, 1907), accessed July 2014, http://www.newadvent.org/cathen/02364b .htm.

70 Treece, *Nothing Short of a Miracle*, xxxiii.

71 Eric Waldram Kemp, *Canonization and Authority in the Western Church* (London: Oxford University Press, 1948), 7.

72 "Canonization," *Wikipedia*, last modified May 28, 2015, accessed August 3, 2015, http://en.wikipedia.org/wiki/Canonization.

73 Ibid.

74 William Smith and Samuel Cheetham, *A Dictionary of Christian Antiquities* (London: John Murray, 1875), 283.

75 Ibid.

76 Ibid.

77 Gregory IX, *Decretales*, III, "De reliquiis et veneratione sanctorum."

78 Apostolic Letter *Caelestis Hierusalem cives* of July 5, 1634; *Decreta servanda in beatificatione et canonizatione Sanctorum* of March 12, 1642.

79 Aimable Musoni, "Saints without Borders: Ecumenical Reflections on the Great Cloud of Witnesses," lecture from the Institute for Ecumenical Research's 47th Annual Summer Seminar, Strasbourg, July 5, 2013, 9–10, accessed August 3, 2015, http://www.strasbourginstitute.org/wp-content/uploads/2013/07/Musoni-The-Catholic-Canonization-Process.pdf.

80 Benedetto Ojetti, "The Roman Congregations," *Catholic Encyclopedia*, vol. 13 (New York: Robert Appleton Company, 1912), accessed August 3, 2105, http://www.newadvent.org/cathen/13136a.htm.

81 Christopher Hitchens, "Less Than Miraculous," *Free Inquiry* 24, no. 2 (February–March 2004), https://web.archive.org/web/20150618090531/http://www.secularhumanism.org/library/fi/hitchens_24_2.html.

82 "How Does the Catholic Church Declare Saints?" Hagiography Circle, accessed August 3, 2015, http://hagiographycircle.com/process.htm.

83 Ibid.

84 Ibid.

85 Ibid.

86 Treece, *Nothing Short of a Miracle*, xxv–xxvi.

87 Andrea Tornielli, "Paul VI's 'Miracle' Receives Medical Approval," *Vatican Insider*, December 13, 2013, accessed August 3, 2015,

http://vaticaninsider.lastampa.it/en/the-vatican/detail/articolo
/paolo-vi-paul-vi-pablo-vi-30603.

[88] Treece, *Nothing Short of a Miracle*, xxxii.

[89] Ibid., xxvi.

[90] Ibid., xxvi.

[91] "Cause for Venerable Sheen's Beatification Moves to Next Step,"
Catholic Diocese of Peoria, accessed Sept. 29, 2015, http://cdop
.org/2014/06/cause-for-venerable-sheens-beatification-moves-to-
next-step/.

[92] "How Does the Catholic Church Declare Saints?"

[93] Paddy Agnew, "Vatican Announces Canonisation of Popes John
Paul II and John XXIII," *Irish Times*, July 6, 2013, accessed August
3, 2105, http://www.irishtimes.com/news/world/europe
/vatican-announces-canonisation-of-popes-john-paul-ii-and-
john-xxiii-1.1454474.

[94] "Report: Pope to Canonize 3 Saints in April by 'Equivalent
Canonization,'" CatholicCulture.org, March 20, 2014, accessed
August 3, 2015, http://www.catholicculture.org/news/headlines
/index.cfm?storyid=20841.

[95] Vatican Council II, *Dogmatic Constitution on Divine Revelation*, no.
4; quoted in McInerny, *Miracles*, 30.

[96] Pope John Paul II, General Audience, January 13, 1988.

[97] Vatican Council II, *Dei Verbum* (Dogmatic Constitution on Divine
Revelation), no. 10; quoted in McInerny, *Miracles*, 30.

[98] Vatican Council II, *Dei Verbum*, no. 16; quoted in McInerny,
Miracles, 30.

[99] McInerny, *Miracles*, 30.

[100] Dom Bernard Orchard et al., eds., *A Catholic Commentary on Holy
Scripture* (New York: Thomas Nelson and Sons, 1953), 211.

[101] Giuseppe Alberigo, *Conciliorum Oecumenicorum Decreta* (Bologna:
Istituto per le scienze religiose, 1973), 57.17–24; quoted in
McInerny, *Miracles*, 122.

[102] Quoted in McInerny, *Miracles*, 122.

[103] McInerny, *Miracles*, 42.

[104] Ibid., 62.

[105] Treece, *Nothing Short of a Miracle*, xxi.

[106] Alberigo, *Conciliorum*, 57.32–36; quoted in McInerny, *Miracles*, 124.

[107] Alberigo, *Conciliorum*, 775.31–35.

[108] Patricia Treece, *The Sanctified Body* (New York: Doubleday, 1989), 33; quoted in Joe Nickell, *Looking for a Miracle: Weeping Icons, Relics, Stigmata, Visions, and Healing Cures* (Amherst, NY: Prometheus Books, 1998), 209.

[109] Treece, *The Sanctified Body*, 10; quoted in Nickell, *Looking for a Miracle*, 210.

[110] Elizabeth Ficocelli, *Bleeding Hands, Weeping Stone: True Stories of Divine Wonders, Miracles and Messages* (Charlotte, NC: St. Benedict Press, 2009), 51.

[111] Ibid.

[112] Ibid., 56.

[113] Montague Summers, *Witchcraft and Black Magic* (Mineola, NY: Dover Publications, 2000), 200.

[114] Ficocelli, *Bleeding Hands, Weeping Stone*, 53.

[115] Ibid., 54.

[116] Herbert Thurston, *The Physical Phenomena of Mysticism* (Chicago: H. Regnery, 1952), 9; quoted in Nickell, *Looking for a Miracle*, 215.

[117] Ficocelli, *Bleeding Hands, Weeping Stone*, 56.

[118] Ibid., 58.

[119] Andrea Tornielli, "Quella 'visita' di Padre Pio nella cella del cardinal Mindszenty," *Vatican Insider*, February 7, 2014, accessed August 3, 2015, http://vaticaninsider.lastampa.it/news/dettaglio-articolo/articolo/pio-pietrelcina-35037/.

[120] Ficocelli, *Bleeding Hands, Weeping Stone*, 60–61.

[121] William J. Samarin, *Tongues of Men and Angels: The Religious Language of Pentecostalism* (New York: Macmillan, 1972), 2.

[122] Ficocelli, *Bleeding Hands, Weeping Stone*, 62.

[123] Ibid., 63.

[124] Ibid.

[125] Ibid., 64.

[126] Ibid.

127 Ibid.
128 Tom Doyle with Greg Webster, *Dreams and Visions: Is Jesus Awakening the Muslim World?* (Nashville: Thomas Nelson, 2012), 139.
129 National Conference of Catholic Bishops, pastoral letter *Behold Your Mother: Woman of Faith*, November 21, 1973, no. 100.
130 Ibid.
131 Fr. Benedict J. Groeschel, *A Still, Small Voice: A Practical Guide on Reported Revelations* (San Francisco: Ignatius Press, 1993), 29.
132 "Modern History Sourcebook: The Apparitions at La Sallette, 1846," Fordham University website, accessed October 21, 2014, http://www.fordham.edu/halsall/mod/1846sallette.asp.
133 Ratzinger, *The Ratzinger Report*, 111–112.
134 Donal Anthony Foley, *Marian Apparitions, the Bible and the Modern World* (Herefordshire: Gracewing, 2002), 68–69.
135 "Testimony of the Right Reverend A. Caillot, Bishop of Grenoble, Following the Report Prepared during the Canonical Enquiry into the Case of Mother Eugenia," in *The Father Speaks to His Children* (L'Aquila, Italy: Edizioni Nidi di Preghiera, 1995), 5–10, accessed August 3, 2015, http://www.fatherspeaks.net/pdf/the_father_speaks_english_v-2005-02.pdf.
136 Ibid., 2.
137 "Teresa de Jesús 'de los Andes,'" Vatican website, accessed August 3, 2015, http://www.vatican.va/news_services/liturgy/saints/ns_lit_doc_19930321_teresa-de-jesus_en.html.
138 "Mary Faustina Kowalska," Vatican website, accessed August 3, 2015, http://www.vatican.va/news_services/liturgy/documents/ns_lit_doc_20000430_faustina_en.html.
139 "Mother Teresa of Calcutta," Vatican website, accessed August 3, 2015, http://www.vatican.va/news_services/liturgy/saints/ns_lit_doc_20031019_madre-teresa_en.html.
140 David Hugh Farmer, *Oxford Dictionary of Saints* (Oxford: Clarendon Press: 1980), 189.
141 "Icon of the Mother of God 'Quick to Hear,'" Orthodox Church in America website, accessed August 3, 2105, http://oca.org

/saints/lives/2014/11/09/103264-icon-of-the-mother-of-god-ldquoquick-to-hearrdquo.

142 Farmer, *Oxford Dictionary of Saints*, 271.

143 Pope Benedict XVI, General Audience, October 27, 2010, accessed August 3, 2015, http://www.vatican.va/holy_father /benedict_xvi/audiences/2010/documents/hf_ben-xvi_ aud_20101027_en.html.

144 "Marian Movement of Priests," EWTN, accessed August 3, 2015, http://www.ewtn.com/expert/answers/MMP.htm.

145 "History of the Marian Movement of Priests," Marian Movement of Priests website, accessed August 3, 2015, http://mmp-usa.net /history_old.html.

146 Maria Divine Mercy's Facebook page, "Jesus to Mankind," had 340,681 likes as of November 5, 2014, https://www.facebook .com/JesusToMankind. The site was shutdown and replaced by other Facebook pages including https://www.facebook.com /Jesus-to-Mankind-Book-of-Truth-156646014383843/timeline/. Accessed September 29, 2015.

147 https://web.archive.org/web/20141107055205/http://www .thewarningsecondcoming.com/the-next-pope-may-be-elected-by-members-within-the-catholic-church-but-he-will-be-the-false-prophet/. Accessed Nov. 7, 2014.

148 Jimmy Akin, "9 Things You Need to Know about 'Maria Divine Mercy,'" *National Catholic Register*, March 3, 2013, accessed August 3, 2015, http://www.ncregister.com/blog/jimmy-akin/9-things-you-need-to-know-about-maria-divine-mercy.

149 Archdiocese of Dublin, "Statement on Maria Divine Mercy," Archdiocese of Dublin website, April 15, 2014, accessed August 3, 2015, http://www.dublindiocese.ie/content/statement-maria-divine-mercy.

150 Congregation for the Doctrine of the Faith, Notification on the activity of Vassula Ryden, Vatican website, October 6, 1995, accessed August 3, 2105, http://www.vatican.va/roman_curia/ congregations/cfaith/documents/rc_con_cfaith_doc_19951006_ ryden_en.html.

151 Congregation for the Doctrine of Faith, "Notification on Vassula Ryden," *L'Osservatore Romano*, December 4, 1996; posted at EWTN, accessed August 3, 2015, http://www.ewtn.com/library/curia/cdfrydn2.htm.

152 Synodical Committee for Matters of Heresy, "Church of Cyprus: Announcement Concerning Vassiliki (Vassula) Paraskevis Pendakis-Ryden," Holy Monastery of Pantocrator of Melissochori website, January 13, 2012, accessed July 20, 2012, http://www.impantokratoros.gr/7F397BAC.en.aspx.

153 "Mystic 'Who Foresaw 9/11' Heads for City," *The Scotsman*, September 6, 2005, accessed August 3, 2015, http://www.scotsman.com/news/mystic-who-foresaw-9-11-heads-for-city-1-1067509.

154 Larry B. Stammer, "L.A. Cathedral Disinvites Christian Unity Event," *Los Angeles Times*, January 10, 2006, accessed August 3, 2015, http://articles.latimes.com/2006/jan/10/local/me-visionary10.

155 René Laurentin, *When God Gives a Sign: A Response to Objections Made against Vassula's Testimony on True Life in God* (Independence, MO: Trinitas, 1993), 33.

156 "The Controversy Surrounding Anne, the Lay Apostle," Women of Grace blog, December 7, 2011, accessed August 3, 2015, http://www.womenofgrace.com/blog/?p=10696.

157 Paul Likoudis, "'Painted by Angels' ... Colombia's Miracle Portrait of Virgin and Child," *The Wanderer*, February 22, 2007; posted at Catholic Culture, accessed August 3, 2015, http://www.catholicculture.org/culture/library/view.cfm?recnum=7471.

158 Philip Serna Callahan, *The Tilma under Infra-Red Radiation*, CARA Studies on Popular Devotion, vol. 2, *Guadalupan Studies*, no. 3 (Washington, DC: Center for Applied Research in the Apostolate, 1981).

159 "Our Lady of Guadalupe: A Message to the Church of the 21st Century," *Embrace Your Greatness* (blog), March 26, 2012, accessed August 3, 2105, http://embracingyourgreatness.blogspot.com/2012/03/our-lady-of-guadalupe-message-to-church.html.

160 "Almost 600,000 Bookings for Turin Shroud," ANSA, February 3, 2015, accessed August 3, 2015, http://www.ansa.it/english/news /lifestyle/arts/2015/02/03/almost-600000-bookings-for-turin-shroud_d67b5314-8ff3-40db-b47b-0893a5cff5c5.html.

161 Ibid.

162 Inés San Martín, "Pope Francis to Venerate Famed Shroud of Turin," *Crux*, November 5, 2014, accessed August 3, 2015, http:// www.cruxnow.com/church/2014/11/05/pope-francis-to-venerate-famed-shroud-of-turin-in-2015/.

163 Joe Nickell, *The Mystery Chronicles: More Real-Life X-Files* (Lexington, KY: University Press of Kentucky, 2004), 242.

164 Mark Guscin, "The Sudarium of Ovieto: Its History and Relationship to the Shroud of Turin," Shroud of Turin website, accessed August 3, 2015, https://www.shroud.com/guscin .htm#top.

165 Mark Guscin, *The Oviedo Cloth* (Cambridge: Luttenworth Press, 1998), 10.

166 "Summary of STURP's Conclusions," Shroud of Turin website, accessed August 3, 2015, https://www.shroud.com/78conclu.htm.

167 "Shroud of Turin Medical Analysis," interview with Dr. Wayne Phillips, *Miracle Hunter*, Radio Maria, February 17, 2015, http:// radiomaria.us/february-17-2015-shroud-of-turin-medical-analysis/.

168 San Martín, "Pope Francis to Venerate Famed Shroud of Turin."

169 M. Sue Benford and Joseph G. Marino, "Discrepancies in the Radiocarbon Dating Area of the Turin Shroud," *Chemistry Today* 26, no. 4 (July–August 2008): 4–12; posted on the Shroud of Turin website, accessed August 3, 2015, https://www.shroud.com/pdfs /benfordmarino2008.pdf.

170 *Compendium of the Catechism of the Catholic Church*, sect. 2, chap. 1, no. 274, http://www.vatican.va/archive/compendium_ccc /documents/archive_2005_compendium-ccc_en.html.

171 Cruz, *Eucharistic Miracles*, 236.

172 Nicola Nasuti, O.F.M. Conv., "The Eucharistic Miracle of Lanciano: Historical, Theological, Scientific and Photographic

Documentation," Eucharistic Miracle of Lanciano website, accessed August 3, 2015, http://web.archive.org/web /20060831022730/http://www.negrisud.it/en/abruzzo /miracolo_eucaristico/tableofcontents.html.

[173] Ficocelli, *Bleeding Hands, Weeping Stone*, 44–45.

[174] Institute of St. Clement I, *The Eucharistic Miracles of the World* (Bardstown, KY: Eternal Life, 2009), 116.

[175] Ibid., 116.

[176] Ibid., 116.

[177] *Decree by the Ordinary of the Catholic Archdiocese of Kwangju*, January 21, 2008, The Miracle Hunter, accessed August 3, 2015, http:// www.miraclehunter.com/marian_apparitions/statements /naju_2008-01-21.html.

[178] See Julia Kim's testimony at Mary's Ark of Salvation, http://www .najumary.co.kr/English/.

[179] Institute of St. Clement I, *The Eucharistic Miracles of the World*, 170.

[180] Ibid., 38–39.

[181] Ibid., 38–39.

[182] Ibid., 38–39.

[183] Cruz, *Eucharistic Miracles*, 235.

[184] "Alexandrina Maria da Costa," Vatican website, accessed August 3, 2015, http://www.vatican.va/news_services/liturgy/saints/ns_lit_ doc_20040425_da-costa_en.html.

[185] Albert Vogl, *Life and Death of Therese Neumann, Mystic and Stigmatist* (New York, NY: Vantage Press, 1978), 2.

[186] McInerny, *Miracles*, 79.

[187] Thomas Head, "The Cult of the Saints and Their Relics," The ORB, accessed August 3, 2015, http://www.the-orb.net/encyclop /religion/hagiography/cult.htm.

[188] L. Garlaschelli, F. Ramaccini, and S. Della Sala (1994). "The Blood of St. Januarius," *Chemistry in Britain* 30, no. 2 (1994): 123; posted at CICAP, December 12, 2000, accessed August 3, 2015, http:// www.cicap.org/new/articolo.php?id=101014.

[189] Nickell, *Looking for a Miracle*, 87.

[190] "Relics of Saints," BostonCatholic.org, accessed August 3, 2015,

http://www.bostoncatholic.org/Being-Catholic/Content.
aspx?id=11478.

[191] Cruz, *Eucharistic Miracles*, 95–99.

[192] Joan Carroll Cruz, *The Incorruptibles: A Study of the Incorruption of the Bodies of Various Catholic Saints and Beati* (Rockford, IL: TAN Books and Publishers, 1991), 27.

[193] Ibid., 31.

[194] Ibid., 40.

[195] Ibid., 43.

[196] Nickell, *Looking for a Miracle*, 92.

[197] Cruz, *The Incorruptibles*, 34.

[198] Ficocelli, *Bleeding Hands, Weeping Stone*, 63.

[199] Cruz, *The Incorruptibles*, 99.

[200] Ibid., 96.

[201] Ibid., 36.

[202] Ibid., 74.

[203] "Miracles of Saint Charbel, a Saint from Lebanon," Charbel.org, accessed August 3, 2105, http://www.charbel.org/saint/charbel/miracles/.

[204] Cruz, *The Incorruptibles*, 294.

[205] Ibid., 106.

[206] Ibid., 294.

[207] Ibid., 106.

[208] Ibid.

[209] Ibid., 137.

[210] Ibid., 106.

[211] Ibid., 137.

[212] Ficocelli, *Bleeding Hands, Weeping Stone*, 46.

[213] Cruz, *The Incorruptibles*, 34.

[214] Ibid.

[215] Ibid.

[216] Nickell, *Looking for a Miracle*, 92.

[217] Rev Charles M. Carty, *The Stigmata and Modern Science* (Rockford, IL: TAN Books and Publishers, 1974), 22.

[218] Michelle Pillai, "Life of a Venezuelan Visionary and Mystic — Jan

214   EXPLORING THE MIRACULOUS

17," January 14, 2010, *Catholic News,* https://web.archive.org/web
/20120307154622/http://www.catholicnews-tt.net/joomla
/index.php?option=com_content&view=article&id=1245:life-of-
a-venezuelan-visionary-and-mystic-jan-17&catid=101:features&I
temid=64.

[219] G. K. Chesterton, *St. Francis of Assisi* (Garden City, NY: Image
Books, 1924), 131.

[220] Thurston, *The Physical Phenomena of Mysticism,* 122–123; quoted in
Nickell, *Looking for a Miracle,* 224.

[221] Mike Dash, "The Mystery of the Five Wounds," November 18,
2011. *Smithsonian Magazine.* http://www.smithsonianmag.com
/history/the-mystery-of-the-five-wounds-361799/?no-ist.

[222] René Biot, *The Enigma of the Stigmata* (New York: Hawthorn
Books, 1962), 20.

[223] Joe Nickell, *The Science of Miracles* (New York: Prometheus Books,
2013), 324.

[224] Ted Harrison, *Stigmata: A Medieval Phenomenon in a Modern Age*
(New York: St. Martin's Press, 1994), 87.

[225] Michael P. Carroll, *Catholic Cults and Devotions: A Psychological
Inquiry* (Montreal: McGill University Press, 1989), 80–84.

[226] Carty, *The Stigmata and Modern Science,* 26.

[227] Fr. Gallifet, S.J., *The Adorable Heart of Jesus* (Roehamton: Manresa
Press, 1897); quoted in Carty, *The Stigmata and Modern Science,* 26.

[228] Michael Freze, S.F.O., *They Bore the Wounds of Christ: The Mystery
of the Sacred Stigmata* (Huntington, IN: Our Sunday Visitor, 1989),
281.

[229] Catherine of Siena, *The Dialogue,* ed. Suzanne Noffke (Paulist
Press, New York, 1980), 5.

[230] Freze, *They Bore the Wounds of Christ,* 198.

[231] Letter to Padre Agostino, September 8, 1911.

[232] Ibid., 197.

[233] St. John of the Cross, *The Living Flame of Love,* stanza 2, no. 12.

[234] Bernard Ruffin, *Padre Pio: The True Story* (Huntington, IN: Our
Sunday Visitor, 1991), 160–163.

[235] Malcolm Moore, "Italy's Padre Pio 'Faked His Stigmata with
Acid,'" *Daily Telegraph,* October 24, 2007.

236 Paul Halsall, "Medieval Sourcebook: Thomas of Celano: First and Second Lives of St. Francis," trans. David Burr, January 1996, "Internet Medieval Sourcebook," Fordham University, January 1996, accessed August 3, 2015, http://legacy.fordham.edu/halsall /source/stfran-lives.html.

237 Harrison, *Stigmata*, 128.

238 Nickell, *The Science of Miracles*, 337.

239 Ibid., 324.

240 Harrison, *Stigmata*, 26.

241 Augustin Poulain, "Mystical Stigmata," *Catholic Encyclopedia*, vol. 14 (New York: Robert Appleton Company, 1912), accessed August 3, 2015, http://www.newadvent.org/cathen/14294b.htm.

242 Carty, *The Stigmata and Modern Science*, 16.

243 Cardinal Bona, *De discretion spiritum* (Rome: 1672), chap. 7.

244 Freze, *They Bore the Wounds of Christ*, 216.

245 Ian Wilson, *The Bleeding Mind: An Investigation into the Mysterious Phenomena of the Stigmata* (London: Weidenfield and Nicholson, 1988), 135.

246 "Sister Magdalena of the Cross — The Nun Who Made a Pact with the Devil," Mystics of the Church, accessed August 3, 2015, http://www.mysticsofthechurch.com/2011/12/sister-magdalena-of-cross-nun-who-made.html.

247 Robert D. Smith, *Comparative Miracles* (St. Louis: B. Herder, 1965), 35.

248 Freze, *They Bore the Wounds of Christ*, 216.

249 Harrison, *Stigmata*, 26.

250 Ficocelli, *Bleeding Hands, Weeping Stone*, 64.

GLOSSARY

Definitions adapted from Catholic Dictionary, Revised, *by Rev. Peter M. J. Stravinskas, Ph.D., S.T.D., published by Our Sunday Visitor, 2002.*

Acheiropoeita (not made by human hands) — a particular kind of icon, typically depicting Jesus or the Virgin Mary, that is said to have come into existence miraculously, not created by a human painter.

Actor — the petitioner or initiator of a saint's cause for canonization.

Apparition — visions of Jesus, Mary, angels, and saints that are investigated by the Church in order to verify their authenticity. Apparitions often contain messages that are considered private revelation, as opposed to the public revelation of Scripture and Tradition.

Beatification — the penultimate step in the process of canonization of a saint, the last step being canonization itself. The act of beatification is performed by the pope after a candidate's life, writings, and teachings have been examined and found to contain nothing contrary to the teaching of the Church or to the demands of Christian perfection. At this stage, the person's heroic virtues are said to be recognized and the Holy Father, with the aid of consultors from the Congregation for the Causes of Saints and especially the postulator of the person's cause, declares the person Blessed, i.e., that the person may be venerated by the faithful. For beatification, one miracle is required, and for canonization, two. At beatification the pope grants the newly elevated Blessed a Mass and a feast day.

Bishop, Metropolitan and Suffragan — the residential bishop of a diocese that is part of an ecclesiastical province, where the primary bishop is known as the metropolitan archbishop.

Blessed — a title bestowed on a deceased person by the Holy See, indicating that the person excelled in virtue and is worthy of public veneration.

Canonization — the Church's official declaration, following beatification and an intensive exploration into the person's sanctity and entire life, that he or she is in heaven and worthy of public imitation and veneration. Seven honors are attached to canonization: (1) inscription in the catalog of saints and public veneration; (2) inclusion in the Church's public prayers; (3) dedication of churches in the saint's honor; (4) inclusion in the Mass and the Liturgy of the Hours; (5) a feast day assigned in the liturgical calendar; (6) pictorial representation; (7) public veneration of relics.

Censor librorum — a person appointed by ecclesiastical authority to read and give an opinion about books that require ecclesiastical permission for publication.

Christogram — a symbol or combination of letters that forms an abbreviation for the name of Christ, traditionally used as a Christian symbol.

Ciborium — a vessel with a cover used for the reservation of the Blessed Sacrament in the tabernacle.

Code of Canon Law — the book containing the universal and fundamental laws of the Roman Catholic Church.

Cult (also Cultus) — in ecclesiastical tradition, the devotion or honor accorded to a deceased person because of his or her virtuous life.

Deposit of Faith — the body of the saving truth entrusted by Christ to the apostles and handed on by them to the Church to be preserved and proclaimed. It embraces the whole of Christ's teaching as embodied in revelation and Tradition.

Devil's advocate (Latin *advocatus diaboli*) — the term denoting the official of the Congregation for the Causes of Saints whose purpose was to present material militating against a candidate's beatification or canonization. The devil's advocate is no longer used; his duties are now fulfilled by other officials in the process.

Ecclesiastical — a term describing something or someone pertaining to or connected with the Church.

Equivalent canonization — an action by the pope to waive the requirement for miracles required for an individual's canonization, thus extending a saint's popular devotion to the universal Church.

Exorcism — the expelling of demons from persons or things.

General Roman Calendar — early Christians followed the Roman calendar of Julius Caesar with a seven-day week and divisions into months. Sunday, regarded by the earliest Christians as the first day of the week and the Sabbath day, was designated the center of each seven-day period. Christian feasts were developed, many of which coincided with Jewish feasts and all of which were set around the high point of the liturgical calendar, the Resurrection. Over the ages, other feasts celebrating the life of Christ, his Mother, and the saints were spread throughout the calendar cycle.

Glossolalia — speaking in tongues; the practice of ecstatic speech among Pentecostal or charismatic Christians.

God's advocate (Latin: *advocatus Dei*) — also known as the promoter of the cause, this is traditionally a canon lawyer appointed to argue in favor of a candidate's canonization; opposes the devil's advocate.

Hagiography — the writing of the lives of the saints or books about the saints. Sources for investigation include martyrologies, liturgical texts, calendars, legends, and biographies.

Heroic virtue — the exemplary practice of the four cardinal virtues (prudence, justice, fortitude, and temperance) and the three theological virtues (faith, hope, and charity) sought in persons considered for sainthood.

Imprimatur (Latin for "Let it be printed") — a canonical term for the permission needed to publish certain kinds of religious books.

Incorruptiblity — the phenomenon through which divine intervention allows some human bodies (specifically saints and beati) to avoid the normal process of decomposition after death as a sign of their holiness.

Indulgences — the remission, either partial or full, of temporal punishment for sins and the resulting satisfaction owed to God. Indulgences may be gained for oneself or for those in purgatory.

Inedia — the mystical phenomenon in which a person relies on no food or water except for the Eucharist for sustenance.

Locution — a form of private revelation in which a mystic receives an auditory message from God, the Virgin Mary, or the saints.

Magisterium of the Church — the Church's teaching authority, instituted by Christ and guided by the Holy Spirit, which seeks to safeguard and explain the truths of the Faith.

Mariology — the study of the Blessed Virgin Mary in theology, which began in the sixteenth century.

Miracle — the transcending of a law of nature, resulting in an unexplained occurrence that glorifies God. A miracle communicates God's will (and is therefore prophetic) and his desire to save humanity (and is therefore salvific).

Monstrance — the sacred vessel (also called an ostensorium) used for the exposition and adoration of the Blessed Sacrament as well as solemn Benediction. The general form and shape of the monstrance is to have a round glass or crystal-covered opening at the center through which the Sacred Host can be seen.

Motu proprio — the common name given to a document written by the pope on his own initiative and addressed to the entire Church.

Mystic — a person who enjoys special gifts given through his or her practice of meditation and contemplation.

Nihil obstat — the approval of a book or writing by an official Church censor before the issuing of an *Imprimatur*.

Normae Congregationis — *Normae S. Congregationis pro doctrina fidei de modo procedendi in diudicandis praesumptis apparitionibus ac revelationibus* (*Norms of the Sacred Congregation for the Doctrine of the Faith on the Manner of Proceeding in Judging Presumed Apparitions and Revelations*) is a 1978 document written by the Vatican's Sacred Congregation for the Doctrine of the Faith (CDF) concerning guidelines for bishops in discerning claims to private revelation, such as apparitions.

Ordinary (bishop) — a person placed in authority over a particular church (diocese) or its equivalent.

Ostensorium — another name for the monstrance, a vessel used to hold the Sacred Host during Eucharistic processions or Exposition and Benediction of the Blessed Sacrament.

Positio — documentation collected by the postulator in a sainthood cause; it provides the biography of the Servant of God and the summary of all the testimonies of the witnesses and documents relative to the future saint's life.

Postulator — the person charged with advancing the cause of a candidate's beatification or canonization, especially in reference to amassing the data on the candidate's life as well as receiving testimony to any possible miracles wrought through the candidate's intercession.

Promoter of the Faith — an official of the Congregation for the Causes of Saints whose duty is to raise all reasonable objection to the canonization of the candidate; frequently called the devil's advocate in the past.

Promoter of Justice — a tribunal official who acts as a prosecuting attorney at penal trials and at contentious trials as well if the public good is at stake.

Relics — bodies of the saints, parts of the bodies, something used by the saints, or objects touched to the bodies of the saints that have enjoyed for centuries the reverence offered by the Church. There are three kinds: first-class (part of a saint's body); second-class (something used by the saint); third-class (an object touched to a first-class or second-class relic). First-class relics of martyrs are placed in an altar when it is consecrated.

Revelation, private and public — divine revelation or public revelation must be accepted with the assent of faith as part of the Deposit of Faith. Private revelation, on the other hand, stems from apparitions or locutions that, although approved by Church authority as "worthy of belief," do not require the acceptance of the faithful. The content of such revelations may never be in contradiction to public revelation, which is found in Sacred Scripture and in Sacred Tradition.

Sacred Scripture — the collection of books acknowledged by the Christian community as written by human authors under divine inspiration and as comprising, with Tradition, the indivisible source of revelation given by God for the salvation of humankind.

Sacred Tradition — the teachings and practices handed down, whether in oral or written form, separate from but not independent of Scripture. Tradition is divided into two areas: (1) Scripture, the essential doctrines of the Church, the major writings and teachings of the Fathers, the liturgical life of the Church, and the living and lived faith of the whole Church down through the centuries; (2) customs, institutions, and practices that express the Christian faith.

Sensus fidelium (sense of the faith) — exercised by the body of the faithful as a whole, this is "the supernatural appreciation of faith on the part of the whole people, when, from the bishops to the last of the faithful, they manifest a universal consent in matters of faith and morals" (*Catechism of the Catholic Church*).

Servant of God — a designation bestowed on someone who is being investigated by the Church for sainthood.

Stigmata — a collective noun for the scars that correspond to the wounds suffered by Christ in his Passion and Crucifixion and appear as abrasions of the skin on certain individuals of unusual personal holiness; usually these marks are external, visible, and painful, consisting of wounds to the forehead, hands, and feet that bleed profusely.

Summarium — the Latin term for a summary document, as typical in a canonization cause, containing all the testimonies of the witnesses and documents relative to the candidate's life.

Synoptic Gospels — the first three Gospels, among which there is an impressive agreement, verbal and sequential. For purposes of comparison, these Gospels can be put into parallel columns. This ordering of materials is known as a synopsis. As a result, Matthew, Mark, and Luke have come to be known as the Synoptic Gospels.

Tradition — see Sacred Tradition.

Translations — a word used to refer to the removal of relics from one place to another, the movement of a feast day, or the transfer of a bishop.

Transubstantiation — a term describing the change of the substance of bread and wine into the substance of the body and blood of Christ, so that only the accidents of bread and wine remain, when consecrated by a validly ordained priest.

Transumptum — in a canonization cause, the transcript of all the acts of the diocesan inquest sent to the Congregation for the Causes of Saints.

Transverberation — a mystical wound in her heart as experienced by St. Teresa of Ávila.

Venerable — the canonical title given to a deceased person who, though not beatified or canonized, has been judged to have lived a life of heroic virtue.

Veneration of the saints — devotion to the saints, who are invoked in recognition of their presence before God and thus capable of intercession on behalf of the living and those suffering in purgatory; they are particularly honored as patron saints because of their example in this life. The reverence shown the saints, called *dulia*, must be distinguished from *latria*, the worship and adoration given to God alone.

Xenoglossy — a mystical gift in which a person is able to speak or write a language unacquired by natural means.